STAR WARS

EVERYDAY

STAR WARS
EVERYDAY

A YEAR OF ACTIVITIES, RECIPES & CRAFTS FROM A GALAXY FAR, FAR AWAY

By Ashley Eckstein

Recipes by Elena P. Craig • Crafts by Kelly Knox

INSIGHT
EDITIONS

SAN RAFAEL • LOS ANGELES • LONDON

CONTENTS

INTRODUCTION

Star Wars entered the world in 1977 when *Star Wars: A New Hope* premiered in theaters, and it has endured for more than 50 years because of what it means to people. It's a spark that lives in our hearts, minds, and souls, and it guides our thoughts and decisions. Whether you're a passionate fan (like me!), a more casual enthusiast, or just someone who loves a *Star Wars* fan, we all have a basic understanding of *Star Wars* philosophy: Life is a balance between the light side and the dark side. We can't always change our circumstances, but we can control our mindsets. Which side are you going to feed? The choice is yours . . . you can choose your destiny!

Star Wars is truly a lifestyle. To understand this statement is to understand what *Star Wars* means to people everywhere. Whether or not you realize it, *Star Wars* is a part of our everyday lives. The lessons that *Star Wars* teaches both consciously and subconsciously permeate our daily thoughts and decisions.

For me, personally, and for millions of fans around the world, *Star Wars* is a story of hope. It's a story of good overcoming evil and a belief that we can always find light, even in the darkest of times. Through its various forms of storytelling, *Star Wars* also shares the story of family and emphasizes that your family is not just the one you were born into; it encompasses your found family as well—friends you meet along the way and strangers who gradually become loved ones you'd do anything for.

Star Wars is a story of love, too. The love that we share with our spouses, partners, parents, children, pets, and friends is reflected in the unbreakable bonds between Sith Lord and son, Jedi Knight and Padawan, princess and smuggler, and even droid and Wookiee. *Star Wars* is a story of adventure as well—it inspires curiosity in fans to go beyond, seek thrills, visit new places, and explore unknown horizons.

Star Wars is wisdom. Quotes from our favorite characters become that inner voice—our conscience, some would say—reminding us, "Try not. Do, or do not. There is no try." *Star Wars* is a belief that we all experience a Force that binds us, an energy that surrounds us. Some use it for good, some question it, and some deny it, but undoubtedly, we all have a sense of this energy that brings us together and connects us here on Earth—not just in a galaxy far, far away. *Star Wars* is a story of new beginnings; a reminder that it's okay to start over, take risks, forge new paths, or walk away from dark situations.

I've been a *Star Wars* fan ever since I was a little girl growing up in the 1980s. I played *Star Wars* in my living room and pretended that our orange shag carpet was the desert of Tatooine. I watched the original trilogy over and over on our VHS tapes, and I joined audiences in the early 2000s to see the prequel trilogy when it debuted in movie theaters. Then in 2006, my life changed forever when I was cast as the voice of Ahsoka Tano in *Star Wars: The Clone Wars*. As a *Star Wars* fan, I felt like I had won the lottery! Not only was I going to be an actor in the *Star Wars* universe, but I also got to originate a new character.

As the voice of Ahsoka Tano in the animated series, I was tasked with bringing my own personality to the character. I was asked to just be myself, and I've been honored to bring my heart and soul to this character for more than 15 years. Interestingly, giving voice to Ahsoka and joining the *Star Wars* universe and community has added a new dimension to my own life. Simply put, *Star Wars* and its fans changed my life. *Star Wars: The Clone Wars* premiered in August 2008, and within two weeks of its debut in movie theaters, I received fan mail from all over the world, welcoming me to the *Star Wars* community and thanking me for being a part of it. Overnight, I gained a family from around the globe, a *Star Wars* family. I instantly knew that this was different than any other role I had ever played and that I was a part of something much bigger than myself. I felt an enormous responsibility to listen to and learn from my fellow *Star Wars* fans, and I wanted to understand everything about the community and culture. All these years later, *Star Wars* continues to play a role in my lifestyle. I have a tremendous amount of love and respect for my fellow *Star Wars* fans, who have greatly enriched my life.

Through this book, I'm thrilled to share some of the many ways that I incorporate *Star Wars* into my daily routine throughout the year. I even enlisted some of my friends and family

to help test out the activities and pose for the photos! I've organized the book by month, with a theme each month that relates to a lesson that *Star Wars* explores, such as hope, love, or friendship. Within each chapter, you'll find evidence-based mindfulness activities to calm your mind, delicious recipes for *Star Wars*-inspired foods, crafts that are a blast to make, and fun *Star Wars* party ideas. Using this guide, I hope you'll discover a variety of ways to incorporate *Star Wars* into your everyday with your friends and family. You might even learn something new about *Star Wars* or gain a different perspective along the way. I'm living my best *Star Wars* life all year long, and I'm excited to share how you can, too!

GLOSSARY OF TERMS & INGREDIENTS

TECHNIQUES

BLOOMING GELATIN

Blooming gelatin helps ensure that the gelatin dissolves easily and creates a smooth, finished product. Using the recipe's specified amount of water and gelatin, place the water in a shallow bowl and sprinkle the gelatin evenly over the surface. Allow the gelatin to bloom for 3 to 5 minutes. You will clearly see the changes as the gelatin begins to absorb the water and swell.

DECORATING WITH ROYAL ICING

Load stiff royal icing into pastry bags fitted with couplers so that it is easy to change tips. On page 182, #2 and #3 writing tips were used to create outlines and fine details. Chewbacca's fur was created with a small closed star tip. To flood the cookies (the term used for giving a cookie a smooth solid surface of icing), place a small amount of icing in a bowl and add water a few drops at time, stirring to incorporate. The icing should be the consistency of pancake batter. Once you have outlined a cookie, creating a wall to hold the flood icing, you can apply the flood with a small spoon or squeezy bottle. Allow to dry completely, 45 minutes to an hour, before adding more details. Sprinkles and dragées are another great way to add details.

DEGLAZING

To deglaze is to add liquid, usually wine or stock, to a hot pan to release all the caramelized bits of food from the pan. These caramelized bits, called fond, are full of flavor and should not be left behind. Deglazing is often the first step in making a delicious sauce.

EGG WASH

Whisk together one egg and 1 tablespoon of water until light and foamy. Use a pastry brush to apply the wash when the recipe requires.

PEELING GINGER

The easiest way to peel fresh ginger is with a small spoon. Simply use the edge of the spoon to scrape away the peel. This technique keeps the ginger root intact, creates less waste, and enables you to easily navigate all the bumps and lumps.

WASHING LEEKS

Leeks are often quite dirty and sandy. To thoroughly clean your leeks before slicing, remove one to two layers of outer leaves and discard. Run each leek stalk under cool water, and gently separate and rinse the remaining leaves. If you'd like, you can also save what you've discarded from the leeks in a sealable bag. Feel free to include other vegetable ends and bits, such as onion and carrot ends, and create a stock to use later.

INGREDIENTS

BUTTER

Butter refers to salted butter, unless otherwise noted.

BUTTERFLY PEA FLOWER

Butterfly pea flower is almost tasteless, and can be used to add color to many foods. It can be found in dried flower or powdered form at health food stores or online. One of the most distinctive characteristics of butterfly pea flower tea, and other drinks that use butterfly pea flower extract, is that it will change color when the pH balance changes. A deep blue tea will turn purple with the addition of lemon juice, turning a deeper shade of purple the more lemon juice is added. Mixed with fuchsia roselle hibiscus leaves, the tea will turn a bright red color.

MILK

The word *milk* in this book refers to dairy milk, unless otherwise specified. Any percentage of milk fat works, unless otherwise noted.

SALT

Feel free to use your salt of choice, unless the recipe calls for a specific kind. Kosher salt is most commonly used throughout the book.

VANILLA PASTE VS. VANILLA EXTRACT

Vanilla bean paste delivers strong vanilla flavor and also provides beautiful vanilla bean flecks without requiring you to split and steep a vanilla bean. Vanilla paste is more expensive than vanilla extract, but in some recipes, it really shines and elevates a dish. If you don't have vanilla paste on hand, you can substitute the same amount of vanilla extract.

EQUIPMENT

SILICONE BAKING MAT

Silicone baking mats can be used with both high temperatures in the oven and subzero temperatures in the freezer. They are helpful when baking because they provide a good surface for rolling out dough and can go from prep station, to fridge or freezer, to oven without requiring you to transfer the dough. Silicone mats are also nonstick and easy to clean.

FRY SAFETY

If you're following a recipe that requires deep frying, these important tips will prevent the possibility of fire:

1. If you don't have a dedicated deep fryer, use a Dutch oven or a high-walled sauté pan.

2. Never put too much oil in the pan. You don't want hot oil spilling out as soon as you add the food.

3. Use only a suitable cooking oil, such as canola, peanut, or vegetable oil.

4. Always keep track of the oil temperature with a thermometer: 350° to 375°F should do the trick.

5. Never put too much food in the pan at the same time.

6. Never put wet food in the pan; the oil might splatter.

7. Always have a lid nearby to cover the pan, in case the oil spills over or catches fire. A properly rated fire extinguisher is also great to have on hand in case of emergencies.

8. Never leave the pan unattended.

9. Never allow children near the pan while cooking.

10. Be sure to keep your hands and fingers away from the pan and any spattering oil: You don't want a Mustafar-inspired accident!

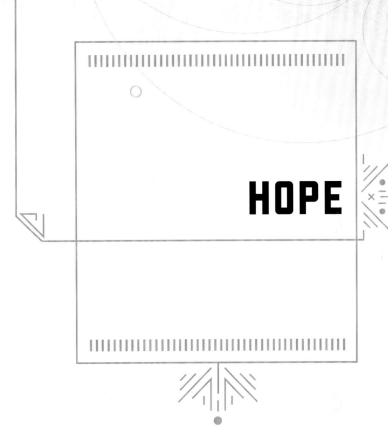

HOPE

"THIS IS A NEW DAY,
A NEW BEGINNING."

Ahsoka Tano, *Star Wars Rebels: "Fire Across the Galaxy"*

"ONE WITH THE FORCE" BREATHING EXERCISE

A new year brings new hope for the future. On a smaller scale, each new day is a gift. Every morning that we wake up, we have the opportunity to be thankful for a new beginning. Before I start each day, I do a simple *Star Wars*-inspired breathing exercise that calms and relaxes my mind. In the *Star Wars* galaxy, we see characters like Chirrut Îmwe and Ahsoka Tano calm their nerves, fears, and worries and slow down the moment with the phrase, "I am one with the Force and the Force is with me."

Luke Skywalker teaches Rey in *The Last Jedi*, "The Force is not a power you have. It's not about lifting rocks. It's the energy between all things, a tension, a balance, that binds the universe together." The Jedi use meditation and deep breathing techniques to ground themselves and connect to the present moment or to the Force.

As you begin this new year, try starting each day with this quick and simple breathing exercise. You can practice this exercise any time during the day when you are feeling stressed or need to slow down, be in the present, and calm your mind.

1. Find a quiet place where you won't be disturbed and close your eyes. If you cannot find a quiet space or are in the middle of a situation that you cannot step away from, that's okay— just close your eyes.

2. Try to block out, or press the pause button, on any thoughts, tasks, fears, and worries that may be racing through your mind. Jedi Master Yoda tells Luke to "Clear your mind of questions." Please be kind to yourself, as this is really hard to do. It takes practice to quiet your mind. The more you practice this exercise, the easier it will become. Do your best to bring your focus to your breathing and your surroundings. Notice what is grounding you. Are you seated on the ground or in a chair? Where are your arms and feet placed? Do you feel secure, stable, calm?

3. Take a deep breath in through your nose for 4 seconds. Place a hand on your stomach and really feel your diaphragm and your belly expand.

4. Hold your breath for 4 seconds.

5. Then exhale from your belly and out through your mouth for 4 seconds.

6. Repeat to yourself out loud, "I am one with the Force and the Force is with me."

7. Repeat steps 1 through 6 for 5 minutes, or until you feel more peaceful and relaxed.

THIS IS A NEW
DAY

A NEW
BEGINNING

"A NEW DAY" WOODEN SIGNS

One of my favorite quotes about hope in *Star Wars* is, "This is a new day, a new beginning." Ahsoka Tano says this in *Star Wars Rebels* when she first meets Ezra Bridger and the *Ghost* crew. Ezra provided a message of hope during a very dark time. As one of the founders of the Rebellion, Ahsoka helped keep that hope alive. I have this quote on my wall as a daily reminder that each new day brings renewed hope.

My friend Kelly, a brilliant crafter, made this craft easy with her step-by-step instructions so you can make this sign, too!

Let's Craft!

1. With the pencil, mark the center of the bottom edge on one of the wooden signs; then mark the center of the top edge of the other sign. The sign with the bottom edge marked is the THIS IS A NEW DAY sign.

2. On the THIS IS A NEW DAY sign, use the bottom edge mark as the center point for the compass. Using the compass, lightly draw a half-circle 2 inches from the center point on the sign. Repeat on the other sign.

3. Mark the arc in the center directly above where you placed the compass. Add six more points on the arc, evenly spaced. Repeat on the other sign.

4. Draw dots for another arc 1 inch from the points you just marked. You should have fifteen points total marked on the sign. Repeat on the other sign.

5. Hammer a gold nail on every point you marked on both signs.

6. Tie the white string to the first point you marked on the sign. Wrap the string around every nail on the inside half-circle, returning to the first nail each time, to create a radial pattern.

7. Wrap the string around a nail in the inside half-circle, then once around the nail in the second half-circle, and again around the inner-circle nail before moving clockwise to the next nail. (This creates both the rays and the outline of the sun.)

Continued on page 16

WHAT YOU'LL NEED

- Pencil
- Two 10-inch-square wooden signs
- Math compass
- Ruler
- Hammer
- Several small gold nails
- Thin white string
- White acrylic paint
- Paintbrush
- ↓ Rebel Symbol Template, page 16
- Black adhesive letters (about 1½ inches)
- Gold adhesive letters (about 2 inches)
- Scissors
- Gold glitter paper
- School glue

TIPS

- Other quotes you can use for inspiration include, "We are the spark / That will light the fire" and "I am one with the Force. / The Force is with me."

- Want to add even more of a *Star Wars* feel? Paint the quote in Aurebesh letters! Aurebesh is the *Star Wars* alphabet, used throughout the *Star Wars* galaxy. See page 133 to learn how to write in Aurebesh.

17. Trace (below) or download and cut out the rebel symbol template at www.insighteditions.com/starwarseveryday.

18. Trace the rebel symbol twice on the back of the gold glitter paper and cut out the shapes with scissors.

19. Glue the rebel symbols in the center of the sun. Let dry.

20. Your new day has begun! Hang the pair of signs vertically to connect the suns and the quote. You can also switch out the lettering for a new favorite quote when the mood strikes!

8. Wrap the string around the inner half-circle to fill in the sun. Tie the string in a knot around the first point, and cut the string with scissors.

9. Repeat the sun string art, steps 6 through 8, on the A NEW BEGINNING sign.

10. On the THIS IS A NEW DAY sign, use the ruler and pencil to lightly draw a horizontal line 3 inches from the top edge.

11. Lightly mark another horizontal line two inches below the first line.

12. Use the lines as a guide and fill the space between the lines in with white acrylic paint. Let dry.

13. On the A NEW BEGINNING sign, use the ruler and pencil to lightly draw a horizontal line 2 inches from the bottom edge.

14. Lightly mark another horizontal line 2 inches above that line and fill the space between the lines in with the white acrylic paint. Let dry.

15. In black lettering, add THIS IS A NEW across the top of the sign that has the string sun at the bottom. Use the gold lettering to spell DAY in the white stripe just below it.

16. In black lettering, add A NEW across the middle of the sign that has the string sun at the top. Use the gold lettering to spell BEGINNING in the white stripe just below it.

REBEL SYMBOL TEMPLATE

VISUALIZE YOUR GOALS

Every year, people set goals with the best of intentions. Unfortunately, sometimes those goals go unmet. Don't worry—it happens to the best of us! When Yoda is training Luke in *Star Wars: The Empire Strikes Back,* Luke tries to lift his sunken X-wing starfighter out of the swamp. His attempt is unsuccessful, and Luke thinks the task is impossible. Yoda then uses the Force to pull the X-wing out of the swamp himself, proving that it is indeed possible with the right mindset. Luke can't believe what he has just witnessed, prompting Yoda to explain, "That is why you fail."

Star Wars teaches us that when we set a goal, we must believe that achieving our goal is possible. Doubt will only open the door to failure. The following is a *Star Wars*-inspired visualization exercise that I find helpful when setting goals. One of my favorite pieces of music is *"Star Wars* (Main Title)". There is something so uplifting, inspiring, and hopeful about the iconic John Williams composition. Just hearing those first few notes makes me feel so excited and triumphant. Find a way to listen to this music and follow these steps.

1. Find a quiet place where you won't be distracted and close your eyes. Pick someplace that relaxes you and makes you feel peaceful. Jedi often go to a dimly lit room and meditate in a pod—what is your version of that? I find that I'm most successful with this visualization exercise when I practice it lying in bed at night right before I go to sleep. However, everyone is different. Maybe you feel most relaxed in nature. If so, find a spot outside, perhaps in a park, on the beach, or even in your own backyard!

2. Play the main theme music to *Star Wars.* There are many ways to listen to the iconic John Williams score. For example, I downloaded the *Star Wars* soundtrack and I also have a playlist on my phone of my favorite *Star Wars* music.

3. While you are listening, visualize yourself achieving your goal(s). Visualize the whole process, working hard toward your goal, and eventually achieving your goal.

4. Repeat this as much as needed until you truly believe that you will achieve your goal.

TIP

I find it helpful to get my goals out of my head by typing them out or writing them down in a journal. It makes them more concrete if you can see them on paper or on your screen. I also always keep a running checklist of goals and add to it throughout the year. Do what works best for you!

AHSOKA TANO'S ROOTLEAF STEW

Everyone needs to eat, including the Jedi! In *The Empire Strikes Back*, Yoda makes a rootleaf stew in his cave on Dagobah. During the winter, I enjoy nothing more than cozying up with a bowl of hot stew. I'm fascinated by the food in the *Star Wars* galaxy, and I've always wondered what that food tastes like. I'm also a foodie at heart, so I had fun working with my friend Elena, a super-talented chef, to come up with my own orange Ahsoka Tano–inspired Rootleaf Stew recipe. Enjoy!

MAKES: 6 TO 8 SERVINGS

Roasted Carrot Purée:

2 bunches of carrots, preferably with greens on (about 1½ to 2 lbs)

1 tablespoon olive oil

1 teaspoon salt

1 cup vegetable broth

Soup Base:

2 stalks of leeks

1 pound cremini mushrooms

2 tablespoons olive oil

One 3-inch piece of ginger, peeled and diced

2 teaspoons salt

4 cups vegetable broth

1 pound fingerling potatoes (multicolored, if possible), cut into 1-inch pieces

1 cup raw cashews

1 bunch rainbow carrots (some purple), cut into round slices about ¼ inch thick

Rootleaf Chimichurri (prepare while the soup is simmering):

Greens from 1 bunch of carrots, thoroughly washed and dried (enough to make ⅓ cup)

Chopped carrot greens

3 tablespoons olive oil

2 tablespoons rice wine vinegar

½ teaspoon paprika

¼ teaspoon coriander

1. Preheat the oven to 400°F.

2. Carefully remove the greens from the carrots and put their stems in water; set aside.

3. Scrub the carrots and cut them into 2-inch chunks. Place the carrots on a rimmed baking sheet and add the olive oil and salt. Shake the pan to coat the carrots.

4. Roast the carrots at 400°F for 25 to 30 minutes or until they are very tender and browning.

5. Transfer the carrots to a large heatproof bowl and add ½ cup of the vegetable broth. Use an immersion blender to purée the carrots, adding more broth as needed until you have a smooth, thick consistency. Set aside.

6. Wash and trim the leeks (see the tip on page 8), removing any tough outer leaves. Slice thinly, through the light green parts only, and set aside.

7. Leaving the stems intact, quarter the mushrooms.

8. Heat the olive oil in a large soup pot over medium heat. Sauté the leeks and ginger until tender and fragrant, about 3 to 5 minutes. Add the mushrooms and sauté another 3 to 5 minutes or until the mushrooms begin to brown.

9. Add 1 teaspoon of the salt and sauté the mixture another 2 to 3 minutes, allowing the mushrooms to release their juices. Use these juices to deglaze the bottom of the pan.

10. Add the vegetable broth and the remaining teaspoon of salt, and bring to a simmer. Add the potatoes, cashews, and rainbow carrots; return to a simmer; and simmer uncovered for 10 to 15 minutes or until the potatoes are tender.

11. To serve: Either stir all the carrot purée into the soup or place about ½ cup of purée into each bowl and ladle soup over it. Top with the Rootleaf Chimichurri (see the next steps).

TO MAKE THE ROOTLEAF CHIMICHURRI:

12. Mince the carrot greens and add them to a small bowl.

13. Add the rest of the ingredients in the list and stir to combine. Allow the mixture to stand at room temperature for about 10 to 15 minutes, for flavors to combine.

A HOPEFUL WATCHLIST

Whenever I need a pick-me-up or a boost of hope, I turn to the *Star Wars* films. For me, *Star Wars* is synonymous with *hope*, so when all else fails, I turn on a *Star Wars* movie or TV show and get lost in the story.

Life gets busy, so if you don't have time to watch an entire movie or show, the following is a list of five of my favorite scenes from *Star Wars* that always cheer me up and give me hope.

"NEVER TELL ME THE ODDS."

At the 35-minute mark of *The Empire Strikes Back*, Han Solo, Princess Leia, Chewbacca, and C-3PO escape from Hoth in the *Millennium Falcon* and must evade a group of Imperial TIE fighters. When they find out their hyperdrive isn't working, our heroes realize they're in deep trouble. Han tries unsuccessfully to fix the hyperdrive but quickly finds himself back in the pilot seat navigating through an asteroid field. It's a life-or-death situation, and the odds are not in their favor. In fact, C-3PO informs Han, "The possibility of successfully navigating an asteroid field is approximately 3,720 to 1." Han famously and confidently quips back, "Never tell me the odds."

I love this scene because it reminds us all that, no matter how bad things are or how much the odds are not in our favor, there's always hope that everything will work out.

VADER'S REDEMPTION.

At the 1:56 mark of *Star Wars: Return of the Jedi*, Darth Vader saves his son, Luke Skywalker, from imminent death by killing Emperor Palpatine. In doing so, Vader sacrifices his own life. Luke rushes to Vader's side to save him and, after taking off his helmet, sees his father's face for the first time. Sadly, it's too late to save the former Anakin Skywalker, but Vader says that Luke did save him: Luke saved Anakin Skywalker's soul.

To me, this is one of the most heartbreaking—and yet hopeful—scenes in all of *Star Wars*. It's the epitome of good overcoming evil: a reminder that darkness might reign, but light and love will ultimately prevail.

THE WRONG JEDI.

In the Season 5 finale of *Star Wars: The Clone Wars*, "The Wrong Jedi," Ahsoka Tano walks away from the Jedi Order. If you don't have time to watch the entire episode, jump to the 19-minute mark and watch until the end. After being framed for murder and wrongly accused by the Jedi, Ahsoka Tano is stripped of her rank and put on trial. She is eventually acquitted of the crime and welcomed back but not before she loses all trust in a system she once believed in. Ahsoka shocked *Star Wars* fans around the globe by deciding to walk away from the Jedi Order.

Being a Jedi was all that Ahsoka knew—it was her entire life—but once her trust was broken, there was no going back. This scene is

devastating, yet hopeful and powerful at the same time. Ahsoka walks away with nothing, but she walks toward the light—toward a new beginning. That act has taught fans all over the world that it's okay to walk away from a situation that is no longer working for them. We might not know where we're going, but the opening quote of the episode gives us important advice: "Never give up hope, no matter how dark things seem."

"I AM ALL OF THE JEDI."

In *Star Wars: The Rise of Skywalker*, at the 1:57 mark, Rey faces death at the hands of Emperor Palpatine; she is outmatched and exhausted. Lying on the ground, gazing up at a war going on above her in the sky, Rey calls out to the Jedi and says, "Be with me." With her life on the line, she calls out a second time and then a third. This time, it works—Yoda, Anakin Skywalker, Ahsoka Tano, Obi-Wan Kenobi, Luke Skywalker, and several others come to Rey through the Force. Now, with the power of all the Jedi, she is able to defeat Palpatine.

This moment is the culmination of the entire Skywalker saga. We can take away so much from this scene, but for me, the ultimate lesson is that we are never truly alone. Feeling alone can be isolating and can play tricks on our minds, but in reality, someone is always there for us, waiting to help. We just have to reach out and ask for it. When you can't find hope yourself, ask other people in your life to help you find it.

"REBELLIONS ARE BUILT ON HOPE."

In *Star Wars: Rogue One: A Star Wars Story*, at the 1:16 mark, Jyn Erso pleads with the Rebel Alliance to undertake a dangerous mission to retrieve and destroy the Death Star plans. Despite being outmatched and outnumbered by Imperial forces, Jyn pleads for the rebels to approve her plan, based on nothing but hope. She famously says, "Rebellions are built on hope."

Hope is one of the most powerful weapons you can possess. Hope can defeat armies and stare down the fiercest opponents. This is one of my favorite scenes to watch when I need a hopeful boost. It reignites that spark inside me, and it's the perfect scene to watch at the beginning of a new year.

HOTH CHOCOLATE SNOWBALLS

Whenever I think of winter, I think of the planet Hoth from *The Empire Strikes Back*. I grew up in Florida and never experienced a true winter, so when I imagine being in a snowstorm, my frame of reference is watching Luke and Han in the middle of a frigid blizzard on Hoth. However, instead of using tauntaun guts to stay warm (ick!), I prefer to get cozy with a nice warm glass of Hoth Chocolate.

We don't see Hoth Chocolate in the *Star Wars* films, but I'll bet someone on the rebel base made a drink like this to stay warm. This recipe teaches you how to make delicious Hoth Chocolate Snowballs. Just place one of these "snowballs" in a cup with the hot milk of your choice and then watch it melt. You'll even find a surprise inside! Next time it feels like Hoth outside, you'll definitely want to make this cozy recipe. It's so good, it'll melt even a wampa's cold heart!

MAKES: 3 HOTH CHOCOLATE SNOWBALLS

7 ounces white chocolate candy melts, divided

6 tablespoons powdered malted milk

About ¼ cup mini marshmallows

About 1 tablespoon sparkle sugar

Special Supplies:

Silicone sphere mold

1. Place the sphere mold on a cookie sheet and have it standing by. In a microwave-safe bowl, melt 5 ounces of the candy melts, 30 seconds at time, for up to 90 seconds. Stir every 30 seconds until smooth.

2. Use a pastry brush to paint a thick layer of the melted chocolate into each mold. Be sure to go all the way up the side of the mold, to avoid any sheer spots. Refrigerate for 5 to 10 minutes until set.

3. When the chocolate has set, carefully remove each half from the mold. (Don't worry if the edges chip a bit.)

4. Have the malted milk and marshmallows standing by. Heat a microwave-safe plate (without anything on it) in the microwave for 30 to 45 seconds, until it's hot to the touch. Carefully remove the plate and cover it with a piece of parchment. Place half a sphere on the plate, rim down. Gently press and twist the sphere to clean up and flatten the edge.

5. Place this half-sphere back on the cookie sheet and fill it with 2 tablespoons of malted milk and 6 to 8 marshmallows. Repeat the process with a second half-sphere, again cleaning and heating up the edges. Gently press the two halves together,

sealing in the malted milk and marshmallows. Use melted chocolate from the plate to close any gaps. Repeat steps 4 and 5 to make two more snowballs. Reheat the plate, as necessary

6. Melt the remaining 2 ounces of chocolate and place it in a pastry bag or sandwich bag. Snip a small opening and drizzle chocolate over the top of each snowball. While the chocolate is still wet, sprinkle it with sparkle sugar. Allow the snowball to set in the refrigerator for 5 minutes or at room temperature for 10 minutes.

7. When the chocolate snowballs are dry, you can store them in an airtight container for up to 3 weeks or wrap them in cellophane bags and give them as gifts.

8. To serve: Place 1 chocolate snowball in the bottom of a heat-safe glass or mug, and fill the mug with 8 ounces of hot milk of your choice. Stir and enjoy.

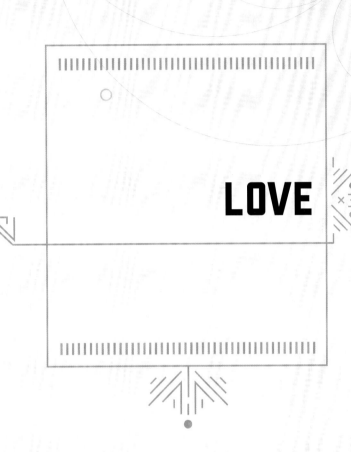

LOVE

"I LOVE YOU."
"I KNOW."

Princess Leia and Han Solo,
The Empire Strikes Back

WHAT YOU'LL NEED

- 4½-by-6½-inch white cardstock
- Scissors
- 3-by-3-inch piece of burlap
- School glue
- Light green cardstock or construction paper
- Light pink cardstock or construction paper
- Black cardstock or construction paper
- 1½-inch heart paper punch
- ¼-inch heart paper punch
- 1-hole paper punch
- White paper for printing or writing
- Valentine's Day treat (such as a piece of candy or a *Star Wars* pencil)
- Tape

February is a month of love, and love is a consistent theme throughout *Star Wars*. Love comes in many different shapes and sizes, from the romantic love between Padmé and Anakin, to the friendship love between Han and Chewie. *Star Wars* explores the beauty and complexities of love and the many forms it can take.

This chapter shines a light on *Star Wars* as a love language for fans of all ages—and there's no better theme for a Valentine's Day card than *Star Wars*! Grogu and the Mandalorian are a "clan of two," but I think you'll agree that Grogu himself is a "clan of too cute"! This is the perfect card to replicate for an entire class of adorable younglings.

Let's Craft!

1. Fold the white cardstock in half, to make a card.

2. Using the scissors, cut a heart shape of about 2 inches in the burlap. Glue the burlap heart to the front center of the card and let it dry.

3. Use the 1½-inch heart paper punch on the light green paper to make two hearts.

4. Cut one heart in half. Glue the two heart halves on both sides of the top of the face heart, with the straight edge up, to make Grogu's ears.

5. Punch two small hearts from the pink paper with the ¼-inch heart paper punch.

6. Punch two small circles from the black paper with the 1-hole paper punch.

7. Flip Grogu to the front and glue his head to the center of the burlap heart. Glue the small pink hearts inside the ears, and then glue the two black circles as eyes on the green heart. Let the glue dry.

8. Cut hearts from the pink paper and glue them on the card to decorate it.

9. Cut a strip of pink paper the same length as the card, and glue it ½ inch above the bottom edge.

TIPS

- If you don't have a piece of burlap, you can use a brown paper grocery bag.

- No heart hole punches? No problem! Use scissors to cut out heart shapes.

- Feel free to come up with other Valentine's Day messages: "Will you be mine? I'm all ears!" or "Be my valentine. I have spoken."

10. Type and print (or hand-write) a Valentine's Day greeting for the card, such as, "We Are a Clan of Too Cute!" Cut out the greeting with scissors, and glue it to the pink strip of paper.

11. Open the card and write the names for "To" and "From." Tape a valentine treat inside.

IT'S A DATE . . .
STAR WARS STYLE

One of my favorite *Star Wars* movies is *The Empire Strikes Back* because of the love story between Han and Leia. Some fans consider the "I love you . . . I know" scene to be one of the most romantic in cinema. We also see Anakin and Padmé sneak away for some alone time on multiple occasions; their love was forbidden, and their secret romance first captured our hearts and then broke them as we watched it unfold during the *Star Wars* prequel films.

If you're a romantic at heart and you love themed dates like I do, the following are some great *Star Wars* date ideas to try with your loved ones.

STAR WARS UNDER THE STARS

What could be better than watching *Star Wars* outdoors at night under the stars? Here's how you can set up a romantic outdoor movie night at home:

1. Find an inflatable outdoor movie screen or seek out a large, light-colored blank wall.

2. Get a video projector, either online or at your favorite local retailer. (Some shops might even let you rent one.)

3. Pick out your favorite *Star Wars* movie.

4. Set up comfortable seating. I recommend using beanbag chairs because they kind of look like Jedi pods. For another fun idea, create a "wampa rug" by setting out a fuzzy white rug and adding some pillows. Anything that is cozy and comfy will set you up for success!

5. Make some *Star Wars*–inspired food. I recommend Hoth Chocolate Snowballs, on page 22, and Dark Side Chocolate Cookies, on page 156.

6. Enjoy the show!

STAR WARS LOVE LETTERS

One the most romantic moments in the *Star Wars* films takes place between Anakin Skywalker and Padmé Amidala in *Star Wars: Attack of the Clones*. Padmé says to Anakin, "I love you." Anakin, who clearly loves her, too, replies, "You love me? I thought we had decided not to fall in love, that we would be forced to live a lie and that it would destroy our lives."

Take some time to write a letter telling the people you love anything you've been wanting to express. What would you write to someone you love? This letter can express your emotions to anyone, such as a parent, a grandparent, a sibling, or a friend. Follow the steps below to create your own *Star Wars* Love Letters.

1. Start by making the Aurebesh decoder on page 133.

2. Using the decoder, on a separate piece of paper, write your love letters in Aurebesh. Just like Han and Leia or Anakin and Padmé,

imagine that the stakes are high and you might not get another chance to tell this person how you really feel.

3. Exchange or mail your Aurebesh love letters.

A PICNIC ON NABOO

Anakin and Padmé have a picnic on the gorgeous planet of Naboo amid rolling hills, green grass, blooming flowers, and a shining sun. This picnic is an opportunity for them to get to know each other better, and they discuss everything from first crushes to politics.

Sometimes we need to step outside our daily lives and immerse ourselves in nature. Having a picnic date with someone you care about is a great way to connect and these steps will help you do just that.

1. Pack a picnic basket. See page 30 for recipes and instructions on how to prepare the perfect picnic.

2. Dress in your favorite Galactic gear! Do you have a Padmé-inspired dress or a Jedi-inspired outfit? Imagine that you are really on the planet of Naboo, and dress for the occasion.

3. Bring a blanket big enough for you and your picnic buddy, whether it's your spouse, partner, loved one, or best friend.

4. Find a relaxing spot in nature to have your picnic. This might be a park near your home or a spot right outside your front door.

5. Put away your phone and prepare a list of questions to get to know your partner better. Spend your time talking and sharing personal details. A few *Star Wars*–inspired questions might kick off the conversation:

   - If you could visit Tatooine, Naboo, or Hoth, which *Star Wars* planet would you pick, and why?
   - Which *Star Wars* character best fits your personality, and why?
   - If you could own one *Star Wars* creature as a pet, which one would it be, and why?

6. After you eat, take a nature walk in the space around you. Anakin and Padmé had fun playing with the animals and running (and rolling) through the hills.

NABOO PICNIC SALADS & EDAMAME WHITE BEAN DIP

If you visited the beautiful planet of Naboo, what would you pack in your picnic basket? Anakin Skywalker and Padmé Amidala go on a picnic on Naboo, and I've always wanted to know what's inside their picnic basket! Naboo is such a green, luscious planet, so I'm guessing that its fruits and vegetables are abundant and delicious.

   I had so much fun working with my friend Elena on the recipes and ingredients for this picnic basket. It's also a perfect part of a romantic *Star Wars*–inspired date. See page 28 for inspiration and instructions on how to plan that for you and your special someone.

Naboo Picnic Salads

MAKES: 4 SALADS, USING 16-OUNCE MASON JARS

Faro:

4 cups water

1 teaspoon kosher salt

½ cup faro

1 teaspoon olive oil

Roasted Red Peppers:

4 small red bell peppers

1 tablespoon olive oil

1 teaspoon salt

Salad Dressing:

¼ cup aquafaba (from the cannellini beans used in the dip, page 32)

⅛ teaspoon cream of tartar

1 tablespoon Dijon mustard

1 tablespoon honey

2 tablespoons white rice vinegar

¼ teaspoon sesame oil

¼ teaspoon salt

Salad:

1 cup cooked faro, see below

1 cup roasted red pepper, see below

½ cup dressing (or more, to taste), see below

1 cucumber, peeled, deseeded, and cut into bite-size pieces

½ cup blackberries, cut in half or quarters

2 cups baby salad greens

4 pepper bowls, see below

¼ teaspoon cayenne pepper

¼ avocado oil

1. Bring water to a boil and stir in the faro and olive oil. Reduce to a low boil and cook for 15 to 20 minutes, until tender. Drain off the excess water and set aside.

2. Preheat the oven to 425°F. Cut off the bottom of each bell pepper, about 2 inches from the bottom. Use a spoon to gently scrape out the seeds and the membrane, being careful not to make any holes in the pepper (these pepper bowls will hold the dressing for your salads). Set the peppers aside.

3. Remove the seeds and membrane from the top half of the bell peppers, and cut the peppers into large chunks. Toss them with olive oil and salt.

4. Roast the peppers on a rimmed baking sheet for 15 to 20 minutes or until the skins are blistered and the pepper is tender.

5. Place the hot peppers in a container, seal the container with a lid or plastic wrap, and let them rest until they're cool enough to handle. When peppers are cool to the touch, peel the skin from each piece and discard it. Cut the peppers into thin strips and set them aside.

6. Now it's time for the dressing. In a medium bowl, combine the aquafaba and the cream of tartar. Use a hand mixer, fitted with a whisk attachment, on high for 30 to 40 seconds until the mixture is opaque and frothy.

7. Add the mustard, honey, vinegar, sesame oil, salt, and cayenne, whisking on high again until the mixture is well combined and thickened.

8. With the mixer on medium, whisk continuously while slowly adding the avocado oil in a steady stream until all the oil is incorporated and the mixture is emulsified. Place the mixture in an airtight container and set it aside.

Continued on page 32

TO ASSEMBLE THE SALADS:

9. Place ¼ cup cooked faro in the bottom of each Mason jar.

10. Top with ¼ cup roasted bell pepper and ¼ cup cucumber, and split the blackberry pieces equally between the jars.

11. Top each jar with about ½ cup greens, being careful not to pack them too tightly.

12. Top each jar with 1 reserved pepper dish by gently squeezing it until it fits snuggly into the mouth of the jar.

13. Fill each pepper cup with 2 to 3 tablespoons of dressing.

Edamame White Bean Dip

MAKES: ABOUT 2 CUPS OF DIP

2 garlic cloves, peeled

12 ounces edamame beans, cooked and shelled

One 15-ounce can cannellini beans, aquafaba reserved

½ teaspoon kosher salt

¼ cup olive oil, plus more as needed

¼ teaspoon celery salt

3 tablespoons freshly squeezed lemon juice, plus more as needed

1. Add the garlic to the bowl of a food processor and pulse a few times to chop it.

2. Add the edamame, cannellini beans, and salt. Pulse to combine and roughly chop the beans.

3. With the food processor running slowly, add the olive oil. If the mixture seems too thick, add a bit more olive oil to thin it out.

4. Add the celery salt and the lemon juice, and blend until combined. Add more lemon juice to taste, as desired.

5. Serve with crudité, pita chips, or toasted lavash bread. Store the dip in an airtight container in the refrigerator.

A LESSON ON SELF-LOVE

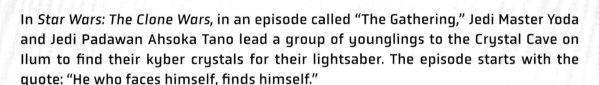

In *Star Wars: The Clone Wars*, in an episode called "The Gathering," Jedi Master Yoda and Jedi Padawan Ahsoka Tano lead a group of younglings to the Crystal Cave on Ilum to find their kyber crystals for their lightsaber. The episode starts with the quote: "He who faces himself, finds himself."

What we watch play out during the episode is a lesson about overcoming the deceptions of your own mind. The younglings had to find their kyber crystal and exit the cave before daylight's end, otherwise the door to the cave would freeze over and they would be trapped. Petro, one of the younglings, did not find his crystal in time and instead of being trapped, he busted through the ice. Katooni, one of the other younglings, questioned Master Yoda, "You... you said we would be trapped." To that he replied, "Not by the cave you were, but by your mind. Lessons you have learned. Find courage you did. Hope, Patience, Trust, Confidence and Selflessness."

This lesson is one of self-love. However, before we can practice self-love, it's important to understand what it truly means to love yourself. The Jedi way is to be selfless, but that *does not* mean you should care about yourself less. (Read that sentence again to make it stick.) Self-love is the act of taking care of yourself, the ability to see your true value, and an appreciation of yourself as you are. Creating a personalized self-love mantra that you recite to yourself can be very helpful in turning your doubts into affirmations. However, mantras work best when they are unique to you. What doubts are in your mind? For example, if you are constantly feeling weak, tell yourself, "I am strong!" I created a self-love mantra, inspired by *Star Wars* and Ahsoka Tano that I say to myself. Feel free to use this mantra below or create your own that is unique to you. The following steps will help you practice self-love:

1. Find a mirror in an area of your home where you won't be disturbed.

2. Repeat the following mantra, or create your own, while looking at yourself in the mirror:

   I am courageous
   I am patient
   I am confident
   I trust myself
   I am selfless
   I am kind to myself and others and
   I will always have hope

3. Repeat this mantra once a day or throughout the day as needed to remind yourself how special you are.

STAR WARS LANDSCAPE CENTERPIECE TERRARIUMS

I love weddings, especially themed weddings! Some couples go all out and have a complete *Star Wars* wedding, while others may want only a touch of a theme, a subtle nod. You can incorporate *Star Wars* into your wedding in so many ways, if you choose to do so. I've listed some ideas here:

- Incorporate *Star Wars* quotes into your vows.
- Utilize lightsabers in your first dance.
- Decorate your wedding cake with a *Star Wars* cake topper.
- Have a live cantina band play *Star Wars* music at your reception.
- Create to-go favors for your guests with Gingerbread Character Cookies (page 182) or Chewie Peanut Butter Sandwich Cookies (page 185).

Another fun idea is to create centerpiece terrariums inspired by *Star Wars* planets for your guest tables. This is such a fun way to include *Star Wars* on your special day! Plus, you can save the terrariums and bring them home with you after your wedding, or you can give them away as gifts to your guests.

Let's Craft!

1. Cover the bottom of the glass terrarium bowl with a thin layer of natural sand vase filler.

2. Fill a small spray bottle halfway with glue. Fill the remaining space with water and shake well.

3. Spray the glue mixture on the sand in the bowl until it's completely covered. Let the glue dry.

4. Fill the bowl halfway with loose moss. Gently tear the moss mat and place it in the bowl so that it completely covers the loose moss.

Continued on page 36

WHAT YOU'LL NEED

- Glass terrarium bowl
- Natural sand vase filler
- Small spray bottle
- School glue
- Water
- Loose moss vase filler
- Moss mat vase filler
- Fake spider webbing or cotton balls
- Small stick with branches
- Foam modeling compound
- Yoda action figure
- Brown acrylic paint
- Toothpick
- Scissors
- Hot glue gun

TIPS

- The steps here are for making a Dagobah terrarium, but you can make centerpieces of all your favorite *Star Wars* planets, such as Crait, Mustafar, Tatooine, Hoth, Jakku, and more! Look for sand and rock vase fillers to get started.

- Add heart details to the terrariums to make them perfect for a wedding table or a romantic dinner setting.

- These beautiful centerpieces aren't just for weddings. They make fun centerpieces for any party, or you can just make one for home decor—no party necessary!

5. Pull apart the webbing or cotton ball, and place it around the moss mat to create a light layer of fog.

6. Break the stick into a length as tall as or barely above the rim of the glass bowl. Glue a little bit of loose moss to the branches of the stick.

7. Press the stick into the moss mat to finish the tree. Squeeze glue around the base to secure it.

8. Roll out a thin snake of modeling foam. If your Yoda action figure has a walking stick, twist and shape the modeling foam into a small heart that's the same size as the handle of the stick. Hot-glue the heart to the handle. If your figure doesn't have a walking stick, form one with a heart handle at the top; let it dry.

9. Paint the walking stick with the brown acrylic paint, and let it dry.

10. Cut the toothpick in half. Hot-glue the cut ends into the holes on the bottom of the action figure's feet.

11. Put Yoda's walking stick in his hand, and then press him into the moss mat. The toothpick supports should keep him from falling over.

WHAT YOU'LL NEED

- White polymer clay
- Clay roller
- 1¼-inch rounded square clay cutter
- Small round circle clay cutter
- Toothpick
- Brown acrylic paint
- Water
- Paint tray
- Paintbrush
- Matte varnish or sealant
- Black string
- Scissors

MAKE YOUR OWN JAPOR SNIPPET NECKLACE

Anakin Skywalker and Padmé Amidala have a connection from the moment they meet in *Star Wars: The Phantom Menace*. They bond during their time together on Tatooine and after Anakin wins a podrace that gives them enough prize money to fix Padmé's ship, Jedi Master Qui-Gon Jinn discovers that the Force is strong with young Anakin and asks his mother for permission to take him back to the Jedi Temple on Coruscant for training. During their trip, Anakin gives Padmé a charm he has carved from a japor snippet. He says he made it to bring her good fortune and so that she will remember him. This necklace remains a prized possession for Padmé, and she carries it with her until the day she dies. Even at her funeral, she holds it in her casket.

A japor snippet necklace is a special gift to give to someone you care about, and it is easy to make! The following instructions help you make your own.

Let's Craft!

1. With the clay roller, roll out the white polymer clay to about ½ centimeter thick.

2. Use the rounded square cutter to cut out a square from the clay.

3. Use the circle clay cutter to cut out two half-circles from the center of both side edges of the clay. Use your fingers to smooth out the edges.

4. Push the toothpick through the top of the snippet, to make a hole.

5. With the toothpick, carve a square shape in the center of the snippet, and then carve two curved lines that stretch from each corner of the center square to the closest corner of the snippet. Carve a small four-pointed star near the bottom edge.

6. Gently shape the snippet into a slight curve (lengthwise).

7. Place the snippet on a foil-lined baking sheet. Bake according to

TIPS

- Polymer clay can damage furniture. Prepare your work surface with plastic or aluminum foil.

- Polymer clays are kid safe and nontoxic, but check the product packaging before you use them.

- Don't worry if your snippet has a rough, handmade look. Remember, Anakin made his charm for Padmé by hand, too!

the polymer clay instructions, and then remove the baking sheet from the oven.

8. Dot the brown paint with the paintbrush near the top and bottom edges and in the center of the square. Paint a small half-circle around each dot. Let the clay dry.

9. Mix the brown acrylic paint with water on the paint tray (about a 1:2 ratio of paint to water). Paint the snippet with the water mix and let it dry.

10. Flip over the snippet and paint the edges and the back side with the water mix. Let it dry.

11. Paint both sides with the matte varnish, to protect the paint. Let it dry.

12. Thread one end of the black string through the hole at the top of the snippet.

13. Tie the string once around the top of the snippet, and then tie a second knot with both ends tied together. Finish the necklace by tying the other end of the string.

"LOVE IS IN THE PEAR" DESSERT

In *Attack of the Clones*, we watch Anakin Skywalker and Padmé Amidala's love story unfold. After their time together on Naboo, they become infatuated with each other and giddy with flirtation. Anakin tries to impress Padmé by using the Force to pick up the pear on her plate, float it over to his own plate, cut it for her, and then float it back to Padmé for her to eat.

To celebrate this lovestruck moment, we've created a recipe for a "Love Is in the Pear" dessert that will leave you floating on air and wanting more!

MAKES: 6 TO 8 SERVINGS

2 cups pomegranate juice

2 cups apple juice

6 small pears, such as Anjou or Bartlett, peeled but left whole

1 cup raw cane sugar

2 whole cinnamon sticks

2 whole star anise

About 1 cup pomegranate arils for serving

1. Combine the juices, sugar, and spices in a large saucepan. Bring the pomegranate and apple juices to a simmer, stirring until the sugar dissolves.

2. Add the pears to the liquid, turning to coat each one. Cover and simmer for 10 minutes or until tender but not soft.

3. Remove the pears to a serving dish and set aside. Bring the liquid to a boil, reduce to a simmer, and continue simmering until the liquid is reduced by about a third.

4. Allow the liquid to cool slightly, about 10 minutes.

5. To serve: Place 1 pear in a shallow dish and ladle sauce over it. Scatter fresh pomegranate arils over the top. This can be enjoyed as is or served over ice cream, with yogurt, or with a dollop of crème fraîche.

TIP

The dish can be served either warm or chilled. You can serve it right away, with the sauce warm, or you can chill the pears and the sauce in separate containers and refrigerate until serving.

JANUARY

FEBRUARY

MARCH

APRIL

MAY

JUNE

JULY

AUGUST

SEPTEMBER

OCTOBER

NOVEMBER

DECEMBER

DISCIPLINE

"YOUR FOCUS DETERMINES
YOUR REALITY."

Qui-Gon Jinn, *The Phantom Menace*

WHAT YOU'LL NEED

- Seven flat, medium-size river rocks
- White and green acrylic paint
- Thin paintbrush
- Paint tray

> "CONTROL, CONTROL! YOU MUST LEARN CONTROL!"

Jedi Master Yoda, *The Empire Strikes Back*

Discipline is all about the ability to control yourself in any situation. It is an important part of Jedi training because a Jedi must be disciplined to learn self-control.

When Yoda trains Luke on Dagobah, he teaches him how to stack stones by using the Force. This is a difficult exercise that requires complete concentration, patience, discipline, and control. Now you can practice this exercise, too! All stones are unique, with different sizes, different edges, and different shapes. To successfully stack them into a tower, you must carefully study the stones and determine how to best arrange them. If you stack the stones too quickly, they could fall.

First, create your Aurebesh Stacking Stones by following the instructions on page 45. Then you can start practicing the task of stacking all seven rocks on top of each other. Feel the Force flow through you, clear your mind, and concentrate solely on the stones.

I recommend making three different sets of stone stacks:

- **Youngling (easy):** The stones have a relatively smooth surface.
- **Jedi Padawan (moderate):** The stones have a bit more texture and variation in size.
- **Jedi Master (difficult):** The stones are all completely different in size, shape, and texture.

You'll need practice, discipline, and control to master all three sets, but you can do it!

TIPS

- You can find river rocks at craft and home improvement stores, but before you shop, take a look outside. Searching for stones can be just as comforting as stacking them.
- You can also make the Aurebesh decoder on page 133 and then use it to translate the letters for *control* or another calming word.

Let's Craft!

1. Wash the rocks and let them dry.

2. Beginning with the smallest rock and then moving to the next largest in size, use the white paint to write CONTROL in Aurebesh with one letter on each rock. To use the Aurebesh alphabet, go to page 133 to create an Aurebesh decoder. Let the paint dry before you continue to the next step.

3. Place a small amount of green acrylic paint in the paint tray. Mix in differing small amounts of white paint in each area so that you have three shades of green on the tray.

4. Paint designs on your rocks. You can add stripes, create swirls, or use the other end of the paintbrush to make small dots—anything you want!

5. Let all the paint dry.

6. Now start stacking! Try stacking from the largest rock on the bottom to the smallest on the top, or test out other combinations as you balance each stone on another.

REY'S POLYSTARCH PORTION BREAD WITH RASPBERRY CHIA JAM

In *Star Wars: The Force Awakens*, Rey must earn food portions by scavenging old ships for metal or other valuable parts. Throughout the *Star Wars* galaxy, many characters eat simply to gain fuel and give themselves enough energy to navigate their training or scavenging. Their food needs to be full of protein and carbohydrates to provide the stamina necessary.

I was fascinated by Rey's portion bread when I saw it instantly rise after she poured the water and powder on it. Rey's exact portion bread exists only in a galaxy far, far away, but I wanted to create my own version of it for you. My friend Elena and I also took some liberties and added our own Raspberry Chia Jam recipe—after all, nothing is better than jam with bread! This recipe provides the right amount of fuel for your training.

MAKES: 12 TO 14 MUFFINS

Raspberry Chia Jam:

2 cups raspberries, frozen or fresh, rinsed

1½ tablespoons chia seeds

About 2 tablespoons coconut oil, for greasing the pan

Rey's Portion Bread Batter:

1½ cups oats

½ cup rice flour

1½ teaspoons baking soda

1 teaspoon vanilla extract

¾ cup applesauce

1½ cups oat milk

2 tablespoons coconut sugar

½ teaspoon cinnamon

1. To start, make the Raspberry Chia Jam. In a microwave-safe bowl, stir to combine the raspberries and chia seeds. Microwave for 1 minute. Stir to break up the raspberries, and then microwave for another 30 seconds. Set aside.

2. Thoroughly grease each cavity of the muffin pan, making sure to come all the way up the side of each cavity.

3. In a blender or food processor, blend all the bread batter ingredients except the coconut sugar and cinnamon until they are fully incorporated and you've achieved a batter-like consistency.

4. Fill each muffin cavity half full of batter mixture. Add a generous tablespoon of the Raspberry Chia Jam into the center of each muffin.

5. Combine the coconut sugar and cinnamon, and sprinkle about ½ teaspoon on top of each muffin.

6. Bake 15 to 18 minutes or until a cake tester (stuck into the side) comes out mostly clean.

7. Allow to cool 15 minutes before gently removing the muffins from the pan with an offset spatula. Top each muffin with a raspberry and serve warm. Allow any extra muffins to cool completely, and store them in an airtight container for 2 or 3 days.

REMOVE DISTRACTIONS

Learning discipline is a very important part of Jedi training, and for living your best *Star Wars* life in general. As Qui-Gon Jinn warns young Anakin Skywalker, "Training to become a Jedi is not an easy challenge." He tells Anakin, "Always remember, your focus determines your reality."

   One of the first lessons a Jedi must learn is to quiet the mind. To use the Force, you must clear your mind of questions and be at peace. But in our daily lives, we have so many distractions: We are surrounded by so many screens, devices, messages, etc. that it can be hard to focus on the task at hand. The following tips will help you remove common distractions from your life so you can focus on your goals.

Keep your devices in one central place. Create a charging hub where your phones and tablets go when they are not in use.

Set boundaries with technology. Limit screen time and set dedicated technology-free time where devices must be put away.

Start your day technology free when possible. Spend some of your first moments in the morning doing one of the mindfulness exercises in this book, such as the "One with the Force" Breathing Exercise on page 12.

Set a goal(s) for the day. Write down or share with others in your life what you will be focusing on that day. This is so they can support you, hold you accountable, and so they know when not to disrupt you.

Create a checklist. Once you complete a task or a goal, check it off your list. You can also make a household chart/checklist so everyone can support each other and hold one another accountable. Encourage one another to create a goal plan. What are the daily steps you are going to take to get you closer to achieving your goal?

Practice doing one thing at a time. It you are doing your homework, only do your homework. If you are playing a game, only focus on that game. If you are building something, only focus on building that one thing.

Plan intentional tech free activities. There are many in this book! For example, have a picnic on Naboo (page 30), make a Kessel Run (page 93), build a droid (page 58) or make Salacious Crumb's Cupcakes (page 83).

Hold yourself accountable. Do not just try to remove distractions. Remember what Yoda says, "Try not. Do or do not. There is no try."

Celebrate your accomplishments. Set a dedicated time at the end of each day to share what you accomplished or what you did that day. Can you check something off your list? Make sure all devices are put away—this is a time just for connection.

Focus on the here and now. Yoda refers to Luke when he says, "All his life as he looked away to the future, to the horizon. Never his mind on where he was, what he was doing." Yoda teaches that a Jedi must focus on the need right in front of your nose and not the future.

FAILURE AS A TEACHER

"THE GREATEST TEACHER FAILURE IS."

Jedi Master Yoda, *The Last Jedi*

When Yoda visits Luke as a Force ghost in *The Last Jedi*, he reminds him that he was supposed to "Pass on what you have learned." He tells Luke to teach Rey lessons of strength, mastery, weakness, folly, and most of all—failure. Learning how to handle and overcome failure is truly one of the most important lessons for a Jedi.

In *Star Wars: The Clone Wars*, "Storm Over Ryloth," after answering a plea from the Galactic Senate, Anakin Skywalker and Ahsoka Tano have been asked to save the citizens of Ryloth from Separatist control. A young Ahsoka has her first opportunity to command a squadron to break through a blockade formed by a Separatist fleet. When the enemy suddenly sets a trap, Ahsoka defies orders and refuses to retreat. She fails to listen to Anakin Skywalker, and she loses many of the pilots in her squadron in battle. Anakin was disappointed in her, and a devasted Ahsoka acknowledges that she failed. They proceed to discuss why she failed and what she can learn from it.

As we've learned in *Star Wars*, we need to learn from our failures, not run away from them. You can do this practice by yourself, with a friend, as a group, or with family. This is great practice for young Padawans, too, as it's very important that we teach children about failure.

1. On a piece of paper or note card, write down a time you failed, or a time things did not go as you wanted them to. Remember, there are no judgments here.

2. If you are doing this as a group, ask everyone to share their failure. If someone does not feel comfortable reading their failure out loud, perhaps someone else can read it for them.

3. Everyone should do their best to answer the following questions below. Try not to use judgement words and only share the facts of the situation.

   • "Why do you think you may have failed?"
   • "What did you learn from your 'failure'?
   • "What would you do differently next time?"

> **TIP**
>
> This should be a discussion. Failure is not something to fear, so make sure this is a safe and judgement-free zone. Let this be an empowering talk about how to handle and process failure.

TRAIN LIKE A JEDI

WHAT YOU'LL NEED

- A large outdoor space with plenty of room to set up stations (your backyard, your front yard, or a local park)
- A backpack to hold your favorite plush animal (If you have a Yoda or Grogu plush, even better!)
- Aurebesh Stacking Stones, page 44
- Ahsoka's Lightsaber Noodles, page 78
- A balance beam, or a similar surface to walk across that is about 6 inches wide and 12 feet long (Use whatever you have available, such as tape on the ground, a curb, a bench, or a log.)
- A kiddie pool, a big bucket, or a large pot
- A variety of change equal to 1 roll of pennies, 1 roll of nickels, 1 roll of dimes, and 1 roll of quarters
- A tennis ball
- At least 20 feet of string (any kind)

As a young girl, I loved watching Luke train with Yoda on Dagobah in *The Empire Strikes Back*. I made my own backyard obstacle course and imagined that I was training to be a Jedi, too, just like Luke.

Many screen years later, in *The Rise of Skywalker*, we see Leia train Rey in the forest on Ajan Kloss. There's something so inspiring about these scenes, with nature as their training ground. The following instructions help you create your own Jedi training course at home.

Start by setting up your stations around your backyard, front yard, or local park. When each station is set up, complete the course one station at a time, as fast as you can. Most importantly, complete the course with accuracy and control. Time yourself while you run the course—improving your time will take practice, focus, and discipline.

Invite your friends to run the course with you. Each Jedi should run the course one at a time while wearing the backpack with the plush inside. Set a starting line for the training course that's at least 25 feet away from Station 1. To start, each Jedi should run to the first station.

STATION 1: Walk across the balance beam (back and forth) three times.

STATION 2: Stack all seven Aurebesh Stacking Stones without toppling any of them over.

STATION 3: Mark off two 3-foot-long sections on the ground. Think of this station like the long jump that track-and-field athletes practice on. Have the participants run and jump over the sections for their Jedi Force jumps.

STATION 4: Fill a kiddie pool, a bucket, or a big pot with water. Add any spare change you have: pennies, nickels, dimes, and quarters. The Jedi should quickly grab 1 penny, 1 nickel, 1 dime, and 1 quarter from the pool. Imagine that you are like Luke, "lifting" items out of the water.

STATION 5: Tie a tennis ball to the end of a string, and hang the ball from a tree branch or similar support. When hung, the height of the ball should be equal to your chest and shoulder area. Use the pool noodle lightsabers to practice your lightsaber swings. The Jedi should swing at the tennis ball and try to hit it five times.

TIPS

- Get creative with this activity! These stations are just suggestions, and everyone's environment is different. What training station can you make in your yard? Incorporate play sets and more jumps, runs, swings, and other actions. Have fun with this activity, and make it your own!

- This is a training course, so I recommend wearing training attire when participating in this activity. Wear something comfortable and nonrestrictive that you can run around in. I also recommend wearing closed-toe sneakers or running shoes.

TWIN SUNS GOLDEN MILK

We already know and love the blue and green milks in the *Star Wars* universe, but I imagine that other colors and flavors of milk must also exist in a galaxy far, far away. When we aren't provided a backstory for the food and drink in the *Star Wars* films, I tend to create my own interpretations. By the time we meet young Anakin Skywalker, he is already a skilled builder and proficient podracer. Living under the hot Tatooine twin suns must be taxing, so I imagine that his mother, Shmi Skywalker, most likely gives him something cool to drink, to replenish his energy.

For this book, I've teamed up with Elena to create a golden milk recipe inspired by the twin suns of Tatooine. I can imagine that Shmi Skywalker might serve young Anakin a glass of this drink after a long day. It's also a great drink to have ready for your Padawans after they participate in the Jedi training course (page 50).

MAKES: 4 DRINKS

1 teaspoon turmeric

1 vanilla bean (see tip, below)

One 3-inch piece of ginger, peeled and sliced

2 to 4 tablespoons honey, or to taste

4 cups unsweetened almond milk

1. In a medium saucepan over medium-high heat, add the turmeric and stir until it becomes fragrant.

2. Remove the pan from heat. Split and scrape the vanilla bean, adding both the seeds and the pod to the pot. Add the pieces of ginger, honey, and almond milk.

3. Return the pan to the stove. Over medium heat, stir to combine the ingredients and melt the honey. Continue to heat the mixture until it just begins to simmer.

4. Remove the pan from heat and allow to cool completely, about 30 to 40 minutes. Strain to remove the ginger and the vanilla pod. Store in an airtight container in the refrigerator for 3 to 5 days.

5. To serve: Enjoy either warm or over ice.

TIP

A whole vanilla bean gives this drink a rich and deep flavor, but 1 teaspoon of vanilla bean paste or 2 teaspoons of vanilla extract can be substituted if needed. (See more tips on page 8.)

YODA'S CAVE CHALLENGE

While training on Dagobah in *The Empire Strikes Back*, Luke is pulled towards a cave that he feels he must enter. He asks Yoda what's inside and Yoda replies, "Only what you take with you." Luke walks toward the cave and puts on his weapons belt. Yoda advises, "Your weapons, you will not need them." Luke does not heed Yoda's advice and takes his weapons anyway. However, what Luke did not realize was that he was walking into his own mind; he failed this challenge because he brought feelings of fear and anger into the cave.

It's important to remember that experiencing feelings like anger and fear is not bad and it does not mean that you have fallen to the dark side. These feelings are natural and we all experience them. It's what you do with these feelings.

It takes discipline to control the thoughts in our minds as they can sometimes be worse than any Sith Lord you might face, taking our deepest, darkest fears, consuming our thoughts, and telling us things that are not true. Learning to silence the negative thoughts in your head is not easy, but I know you can do this.

For this exercise, identify a challenge in your own life, such as a big meeting or interview, an important test at school, a big game or tournament, or maintaining a relationship with a family member or friend. What is something that causes you to have feelings of fear, anger or stress?

1. First, draw a cave on a piece of paper, and inside the cave, write down the challenge that you've identified and all of the thoughts and feelings you are having about this challenge. For me, this was the very first exercise I did when I started to write this book. I had so many fears, that when I first sat down to start writing, I had surrounded myself with doubt. This was the challenge inside my cave.

2. Next, think about how you are going to face that challenge, and what you are going to bring into the cave with you. In my example, I became so consumed with doubt about my writing skills that I couldn't actually start writing. I had to take a break and I re-watched *The Empire Strikes Back* for the cave scene with Yoda and Luke. I realized that my writing room was my cave and I needed to go back in my room armed with confidence and kindness toward myself.

3. Now that you're inside the cave, write down all the things, actions, and emotions that you will bring with you. I wrote down that I wanted to bring a positive attitude and an action plan. I decided to break the book down one section at a time, so it wasn't as overwhelming.

4. A big part of what you take in with you is your preparation. Luke was not ready to face his challenge. He did not have enough training and he had not prepared. Think to yourself: Did you do your homework? Did you study? Did you practice? Did you train enough? I was doubting my own knowledge. However, I found out that I really enjoyed researching my ideas and re-watching *Star Wars*. Facing my fear actually turned out to be a lot of fun!

TIP

Even though this is a mental exercise, it can be helpful to have a physical reminder. When it comes time to face your challenge, create something that you can physically take with you. For example, I made a little green note card in the shape of Yoda's head that I put on my wall to remind me to breathe and be calm, patient, positive, and at peace.

FRIENDSHIP

"THE REPUBLIC COULDN'T HAVE ASKED FOR BETTER SOLDIERS, NOR I A BETTER FRIEND."

Ahsoka Tano, *Star Wars: The Clone Wars*, "Shattered"

A DROID BEST FRIEND

The relationship between *Star Wars* droids and those they serve is a special one. R2-D2, C-3PO, BB-8, Chopper, D-O, and K-2SO have all saved the day on many adventures, and the bonds they have with our favorite *Star Wars* heroes is unbreakable.

R2-D2 is one of my favorite characters because he is truly the unsung hero of *Star Wars*. He's always there to deliver important messages, store and deliver secret plans, fix ships, create distractions, shut down trash compactors, light fires, put out fires, open doors, fix hyperdrives, break chains, cut through traps, and toss lightsabers at exactly the right time—whew! R2-D2 has pretty much saved everyone's life at some point. He's also a trusted friend to so many characters in the *Star Wars* universe. The Skywalker saga would have turned out completely different if R2-D2 hadn't been in the picture.

I've always wanted to have my own droid; maybe one day, I'll learn how to build my own fully functioning mechanical droid. In the meantime, and thanks to Kelly, I've learned how to build my own nonmechanical droid companion out of recycled materials. Using the following instructions, you can, too!

Continued on page 60

TIPS

- Make your own version of a favorite droid, such as R2-D2 or Clink from *Star Wars: The Bad Batch*, or design your own!

- If you don't have plastic eggs, check the recycling bin for large sports drink caps or other round pieces.

- Feel free to use school glue instead of hot glue when making this craft with kids.

Let's Craft!

1. If you're using a toilet paper roll for the body, cut it in half. If you're using a spray can cap, keep it as is.

2. Separate the plastic egg pieces. Glue the round bottom piece to the top of the tube or cap to make the droid's head.

3. Glue the googly eyes to the round head piece to make the droid's eyes and lights.

4. Cut small strips of cardboard and plastic packaging in various rectangular shapes no larger than 2 inches long.

5. Glue the strips and googly eyes to the droid's body for its panels and other components.

6. Cut the jumbo craft stick in half.

7. Cut both straws into four equal pieces. Glue two pieces per side around the straight edge of the craft stick pieces.

8. Glue the craft stick pieces to the droid's body for the legs, rounded side up.

9. It's time to paint! Begin by painting the main colors: typically, silver for the head and white for the body and legs.

10. Paint the components: The googly eyes on the head are black, and the pieces on the body can be silver or white. Make the droid your own!

11. Add details around the head with blue paint (or with a different color).

12. When the paint is dry, add weathering as desired by dry brushing silver acrylic paint on the edges of all "metal" pieces. Add more dirt and weathering by dry brushing black acrylic paint on the body and legs.

REACH OUT

From Luke and Han, to Captain Rex and Ahsoka, to Rey and Finn, *Star Wars* has some pretty iconic friendships—friends who go on adventures together, friends who are always there for each other, friends who always have each other's back, and friends who become family. *Star Wars* teaches us that our family is not just the one we're born with—it's also those we choose to be a part of our lives.

In *The Last Jedi*, Rey and Kylo Ren are able to connect through the Force and communicate even though they aren't physically near each other. Rey had traveled to the island of Ahch-To to train with Luke Skywalker and to seek answers about who she is and where she has come from. Her hope had hit rock bottom after Luke rejected her and didn't answer her questions. Devastated, Rey says that she feels alone. Kylo says to her, "You're not alone." Rey then responds, "Neither are you."

The lesson here is that you're never really alone. One of the worst feelings in the world is to feel invisible, as if no one sees you or cares about you. But thanks to the many ways we can connect with our friends and loved ones, it's easier now than ever to feel supported.

Today, reach out to someone you care about, and let one or more loved ones know that they're not alone and that you're thinking of them. Use the Force to send a message—or, in this case, write a letter, send an email or text, or call on the phone.

CARBONITE CLAY MASKS

WHAT YOU'LL NEED

- 4 tablespoons bentonite clay
- 1 tablespoon activated charcoal
- 4 tablespoons apple cider vinegar
- 4 tablespoons filtered water

Optional:

- 2 tablespoons raw honey
- 2 drops of your favorite essential oil (I use tea tree oil because it has a cooling effect, kind of like carbonite)

In one of the most memorable scenes in *The Empire Strikes Back*, Darth Vader freezes Han Solo in carbonite. Not too many positives generally go along with being frozen in carbonite, but one I can imagine is that it might be really good for the skin. (I'm not certain, but if you're frozen in time, it must be good for something!)

I love having my friends over for a low-key night at home, so I created this DIY Carbonite Clay Mask to make with my friends—and yours, too! This simple, all-natural clay mask is meant to soothe and detox your skin. For the perfect *Star Wars* night in, I recommend creating these masks and baking Salacious Crumb's Bake Shop Cupcakes on page 83 for a fun treat.

1. Add the bentonite clay and activated charcoal into a small mixing bowl, and mix well.

2. Add the apple cider vinegar and water, and stir the mixture with a small whisk until the ingredients are combined.

3. Add the optional honey or essential oil, if you choose.

4. Make sure the mask has a paste consistency; then use your fingers to apply the mask to your clean, dry face.

5. Let the mask stay on your face for about 20 minutes.

6. Rinse your face with warm water and apply your favorite moisturizer.

A *STAR WARS* BIRTHDAY PARTY

As a *Star Wars* fan, having a *Star Wars* birthday party is pretty much a rite of passage. You can incorporate *Star Wars* into your special day in so many fun ways. The following are a couple different themes for planning your next party.

A Jedi Training Party

All young Padawans want a Jedi Training Party! It's the perfect party for a group of kids—or even kids at heart.

1. Everyone can start by making their own Jedi robes. You can find the instructions on page 127.

2. Then get everyone together to make their own pool noodle lightsabers. You can find the crafting instructions for Ahsoka's Lightsaber Noodles on page 78.

3. When it's time to refuel, have the partygoers create their own Jedi Training Snack Box, inspired by Luke's rations box that he pulls out of his backpack on Dagobah (page 123). Stage a table with various snacks on it, and have your Padawans fill up their own boxes with their favorite snacks.

4. After a snack, everyone can participate in the Train Like a Jedi course, on page 50. Be sure to adjust the stations based on the age and mobility level of the Padawans.

5. Finally, have everyone wind down and connect with the Force by practicing the "One with the Force" Breathing Exercise on page 12.

Continued on page 64

A Rebel Alliance Party

Before the Resistance, there was the Rebel Alliance: a scrappy group of rebels, including Luke Skywalker, Princess Leia, and Han Solo, who defied all odds to blow up the Death Star (both the first and the second!) and defeat the Galactic Empire. To celebrate their achievement, plan a party that is perfect for rebels of all ages! What *Star Wars* fan wouldn't want to do a Kessel Run at home?

1. Everyone can start by making their own *Millennium Falcon* cutout. Use the template on page 171 to trace a *Millennium Falcon* on a gray piece of construction paper or download the template online at www.insighteditions.com/starwarseveryday. Cut out the *Millennium Falcon* and, using a safety pin, attach it to the back of each guest's shirt, just like a runner's bib.

2. While wearing their *Millennium Falcon*, everyone participates in a Kessel Run. Follow the instructions on page 93 for setting up your own Kessel Run at home.

3. Set up the Pin the Buns on Leia activity below, and have your younglings use the Force to find Princess Leia.

4. Make a Death Star piñata by following the instructions on page 80, and have your little rebels destroy the Death Star.

5. Complete the party with a Birthday Celebration Ceremony with Cookies for Wookiees (& Milk)! You can find the recipe on page 181.

WHAT YOU'LL NEED

- 🔽 Princess Leia template
- 1 sheet of sand-colored scrapbook paper
- Scissors
- 1 sheet of brown cardstock or construction paper
- Ruler
- Pencil
- School glue
- 1 sheet of black cardstock or construction paper
- White cardstock or construction paper
- Hole punch
- Masking tape

Pin the Buns on Leia

Princess Leia was the original self-rescuing hero, and her fashion sense made her the ultimate trendsetter. Leia's cinnamon bun–inspired hairstyle is definitely iconic. Anytime someone wears a hairstyle of two side buns, it's instantly recognizable as Leia's. This fun and simple party game is just like Pin the Tail on the Donkey. Follow the instructions on the next page for this fun party game.

Let's Craft!

1. Download the Princess Leia template from www.insighteditions.com/starwarseveryday. Cut out all shapes from the template. Trace the largest circle on the sand-colored paper. Cut out the circle with the scissors.

2. Trace the hair shape on the brown paper, and cut it out. Glue it in place at the top of the head.

3. Trace the hair bun shape twice on the brown paper, and cut out the circles with the scissors.

4. On the black paper, trace and cut out two eyes and four small triangles for eyelashes.

5. Glue two eyelashes to each black circle.

6. Flip the black circles so that the eyelashes are in the back, and glue the eyes to Leia's face.

7. On the white paper, use the hole punch to cut out two small circles.

8. Glue one small white circle to each eye, to make the light reflections.

9. Trace the smallest circle on the sand-colored paper and cut it out. Glue it in the middle to make Leia's nose.

10. On the black paper, trace the larger triangle and cut it out to make Leia's mouth. Glue it below her nose.

11. Stick pieces of rolled-up masking tape to the back of Leia's face, and stick it to your wall.

12. Stick pieces of rolled-up masking tape to the two brown buns, and you're ready to play!

TIP

Masking tape is safe for the wall and shouldn't peel off any paint when removed. Don't use duct tape!

STAR WARS PARTY FOODS

Every time I watch *Star Wars* and see a scene with food in it, I always wonder, "What does that food taste like?" I like to take some liberties and use my imagination when it comes to creating *Star Wars*–inspired foods, and that's what this next section is all about!

I'm part Italian, so it's in my blood to want share my love of food with my favorite people. When I'm throwing a *Star Wars* party to just getting together with friends, it's always fun to have *Star Wars*–inspired foods. *Star Wars* food with *Star Wars* friends is definitely the perfect combination! The following finger foods and drinks are perfect for fans of all ages.

Bantha Surprise Burger Bites

Wookiees are known to whip up some Bantha Surprise for special occasions, such as Life Day. I was curious to figure out what Bantha Surprise actually tasted like, so Elena and I put our minds together and came up with our own bite-size version that's perfect for parties. I love this dish, and I hope you enjoy it, too!

MAKES: 20 BURGER BITES

Tempura Batter:

2 quarts neutral oil for frying, such as canola or peanut oil

1 cup brown rice flour, plus more for dusting

1 tablespoon cornstarch

1 teaspoon salt

½ teaspoon baking soda

½ teaspoon Chinese five-spice powder

1 ⅓ cups sparkling water, chilled

½ cup gluten-free panko breadcrumbs

Meatballs:

16 ounces bacon, chopped

½ cup minced shallot (approximately 1 small shallot)

3½ pounds hamburger

2 teaspoons salt

Freshly ground black pepper

1 cup gluten-free panko

1½ teaspoons cayenne

1½ teaspoons nutmeg

Mustard Sauce:

2 tablespoons mirin

1 tablespoon Dijon mustard

1 tablespoon Worcestershire sauce

1 tablespoon honey

1. In a large bowl, combine all the tempura batter ingredients except for the water and panko. Refrigerate until needed.

2. For the mustard sauce, combine all the ingredients in a small serving bowl, and mix thoroughly. Set aside for step 7.

3. To start the meatballs, in a medium skillet over medium–high heat, cook the bacon until all the fat is rendered off, between 5 and 10 minutes. Remove the bacon from the pan and allow it to drain on a paper towel—lined plate.

4. Reserve 2 tablespoons of the bacon fat and return the pan to heat. Sauté the shallots for 2 to 3 minutes or until translucent. Remove from heat and allow to cool, about 5 minutes.

5. Preheat the oven to 425°F. Mix together the hamburger, salt, pepper, bacon, shallots, bacon fat, and panko until well combined.

6. Form into 20 equal-size meatballs and place on a rimmed baking sheet lined with foil.

7. Bake for 12 to 15 minutes until internal temperature reads 150°F. The meatballs will continue to cook during the frying process.

8. In a deep skillet or Dutch oven, over medium-high heat, bring the oil up to 365°F.

9. Slowly add the sparkling water to the tempura mix, stirring gently until just combined. Add the ½ cup of panko and stir to combine.

10. Dip each meatball in the batter and fry for 2 to 3 minutes or until golden brown, turning gently if needed. Remove the meatballs to a rack or paper towel—lined plate to drain.

11. Serve with the mustard sauce.

Jawa Juice

Obi-Wan orders some Jawa Juice at Dex's Diner in *Attack of the Clones*. We don't actually get to see what this drink looks like, so Elena and I created a recipe that we think Obi-Wan Kenobi himself would enjoy! (Note: This drink might be more for an adult palette, but it's kid friendly, too!)

MAKES: 6 DRINKS

Juice:
4 cups unsweetened rice milk
½ cup golden brown sugar
1 teaspoon tamarind concentrate
1 whole cinnamon stick

Cinnamon Sugar:
¼ cup sugar
1 tablespoon cinnamon

1. In a pitcher or container that can hold at least 6 cups of liquid, combine the rice milk, brown sugar, and tamarind concentrate. Stir vigorously until the sugar is dissolved.

2. Add the cinnamon stick. Seal the container with a lid or plastic wrap, and refrigerate for 4 hours or overnight.

3. Mix the sugar and cinnamon to create the cinnamon sugar mixture, and store in an airtight container.

4. Serve over crushed ice with a sprinkle of the cinnamon sugar mixture on top.

Tauntaun Tenders

No matter how old I get, one of my favorite foods will always be chicken tenders. This kid-friendly staple is one of my go-to comfort foods, and it got me thinking about what the equivalent of a chicken tender might be in a galaxy far, far away. My answer? A Tauntaun Tender! Tauntauns might smell really bad on the inside, but we've managed to make a delicious recipe for Tauntaun Tenders that would warm our heroes' bellies on a cold day on Hoth.

MAKES: 6 SERVINGS AS AN ENTRÉE, OR UP TO 10 SERVINGS AS AN APPETIZER

Marinade:

2 cups buttermilk

1 teaspoon garlic powder

½ teaspoon turmeric

1 tablespoon dried chives

2 teaspoons kosher salt

3 pounds chicken breast, cut into strips about 1½ by 3 inches

About 1 tablespoon vegetable oil

Chicken Coating:

6 cups puffed rice cereal

2 teaspoons garlic powder

2 teaspoons paprika

2 teaspoons kosher salt

Sauce:

1 cup Greek yogurt

2 tablespoons mayonnaise

1 teaspoon Worcestershire sauce

1 teaspoon garlic powder

2 teaspoons dried chives

½ teaspoon paprika

½ teaspoon of turmeric

½ teaspoon salt

Fresh ground black pepper to taste

1. Mix together all the marinade ingredients in a container that can seal well. Add the chicken strips, seal the container, and shake gently over the sink to completely coat the chicken. Let the chicken marinade stand for 15 minutes.

2. While the chicken is marinating, lightly oil two baking sheets. Preheat the oven and baking sheets to 400°F.

3. In the bowl of a food processor, combine 3 cups of the rice cereal and all the spices for the coating. Pulse to combine and break down the cereal until it's a coarse, sandlike texture.

4. In a 9-by-13-inch glass baking dish, combine the chicken coating mixture with the remaining whole cereal, and stir to combine.

5. Remove the chicken strips one piece at a time, allowing the excess marinade to drip off, and press the chicken into the coating mixture. Turn the chicken over to coat both sides. Leave the chicken in the dredging station, and continue coating more chicken strips until the station is full.

6. When you have a full pan of coated chicken strips, open the oven and carefully add the strips to a prepared baking sheet.

7. Coat the remaining chicken and add it to the second baking sheet.

8. Bake at 400°F for 20 to 25 minutes or until a meat thermometer reaches 165°F.

9. In a medium bowl add all the ingredients and whisk together to combine. This can be used right away but is even better refrigerated for a least 30 minutes before serving so the flavors can meld. Refrigerate until serving.

Tatooine Purple Juice

When Anakin and Padmé visit Tatooine to find Anakin's mother, Shmi Skywalker, in *Attack of the Clones*, they meet Anakin's stepfather, Cliegg Lars; Anakin's stepbrother, Owen Lars; and Owen's girlfriend, Beru. While sitting at their table, Beru serves them a purple juice. I've always wondered what this drink tastes like, so Elena and I made our best guess. We decided to take it a step further and add some refreshing ice cubes for a hot day on Tatooine. This drink is perfect for younglings and Padawans alike!

MAKES: 4 DRINKS

2 cups blueberries

4 cups coconut water, divided

1 cup purple grape juice

1 teaspoon vanilla bean paste

1 pint vanilla ice cream (optional)

Special Supplies:

Small ice cube mold

1. Rinse blueberries and gently smash half of them.

2. In the ice cube mold, press 2 blueberries, one whole and one smashed, into the mold. Cover with about 1 cup of the coconut water. Place the mold in the freezer overnight and allow the contents to freeze solid.

3. Meanwhile, combine the remaining coconut water, grape juice, and vanilla bean paste. Stir to combine, and refrigerate until serving.

4. To serve: Fill each glass with ice cubes, and cover the ice with the grape juice mixture. If you're using ice cream, leave 3 inches of clearance at the top of the glass for the scoop. Enjoy!

CELEBRATION

"MAY THE FORCE
BE WITH YOU."

Obi-Wan Kenobi, *A New Hope*

MAY THE 4TH MOVIE NIGHT

From school graduations to the beginning of summer, May typically kicks off a season of celebrations. However, for *Star Wars* fans, May has become a very important month because it's when we celebrate our unofficial holiday, May the 4th! This is a day when we all come together and celebrate what it means to be a *Star Wars* fan, so gather your friends and family and celebrate the *Star Wars* community you've built.

My favorite activity for May the 4th is hosting a *Star Wars* movie night. I love to invite everyone over to my house for a fun, Force-filled night of celebrating this iconic franchise that we love so much! Here are some ideas on how to host the perfect movie night:

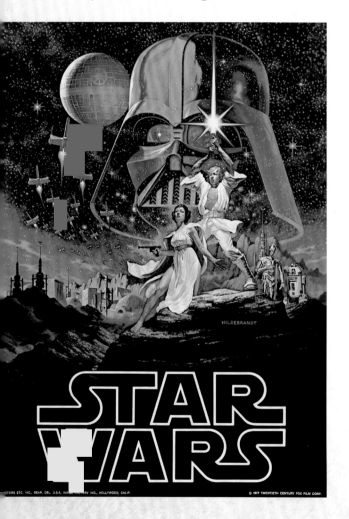

Ask everyone to show up dressed like their favorite *Star Wars* character. This can be an entire costume or just an "inspired by" look! See page 152 for how to dress for the dark side, and see page 127 for how to make your own Jedi robe.

Create your own Dex's Diner and *Star Wars*– inspired food. I highly recommend the Bantha Surprise Burger Bites on page 66, the Tauntaun Tenders on page 69, and Jabba's "Frog" Legs on page 75.

Make a *Star Wars*–themed drinks station. We've created several delicious drink recipes for this book, all of which are perfect to serve at a party on May the 4th; you can find them on page 68 and 70. We even created a recipe for this special occasion: Check out the Yoda Punch recipe on page 77.

Play *Star Wars* trivia. Set up a trivia game with your guests using the *Star Wars* trivia ideas on page 121. This can be an individual game or one that you play in groups. The individual winner or winning group of your trivia game gets to pick the *Star Wars* movie you watch.

JABBA'S "FROG" LEGS

In *Return of the Jedi*, we see that the notorious gangster Jabba the Hutt is no stranger to celebrations, and he certainly knows how to throw a party in his palace. One of Jabba's favorite snacks appears to be a Klatooine paddy frog, which we see him eat in the movie. He even has a bowl of the frogs right next to his throne! This dish also makes the perfect party food for a May the 4th party. (Note: No frogs were harmed in the making of this recipe.)

MAKES: 6 SERVINGS AS AN ENTRÉE, OR UP TO 10 SERVINGS AS AN APPETIZER
BRINING TIME: 2 TO 6 HOURS

8 cups (or 2 quarts) cool water

½ cup kosher salt

1 teaspoon wasabi powder

3½ to 4 pounds chicken wings or drumettes

Sauce:

1 tablespoon olive oil

1 teaspoon sesame oil

1 small onion, diced

2 to 3 serrano chiles, destemmed, seeded, and diced

7 ounces salsa verde or tomatillo-based salsa

7 ounces mild green chilies, diced

½ tablespoon apple cider vinegar

2 tablespoons honey

¼ cup vegetable oil

1. In a large pot with a lid, combine the water, kosher salt, and wasabi powder, and stir until the salt dissolves. Add the chicken wings, cover, and refrigerate for at least 2 hours (up to 6 hours).

2. While the chicken is brining, make the sauce. In a medium saucepan, heat the olive oil and sesame oil. Add the onions and serrano chilies, and sauté, stirring frequently until soft and starting to brown. Add the salsa verde, canned green chilies, apple cider vinegar, and honey. Stir to combine. Bring to a boil, reduce to a simmer, and continue to cook for 10 to 15 minutes, stirring frequently. When the sauce mixture has reduced and thickened, remove from heat.

3. Use an immersion blender to blend the mixture into a smooth sauce. Set aside. Preheat the oven and 2 rimmed baking pans to 425°F.

4. Line a rimmed baking pan with paper towels. Remove the chicken wings from the brine and rest them on the prepared baking pan. Pat dry.

5. Toss the chicken in the vegetable oil and split it between the two hot baking pans. Bake for 15 to 20 minutes or until the internal temperature of the thick part of a drumstick reaches 160°. Have a large heat-proof bowl standing by.

6. Working with half of the wings at a time, put about ½ cup of sauce into the bowl and toss the wings in the sauce.

7. Return the wings to the oven and repeat with the second pan of wings. Cook for another 10 minutes until the chicken is well glazed and the temperature is at least 165°F.

YODA PUNCH

Yoda Punch is inspired by its namesake, Jedi Master Yoda. This drink really packs a punch with a mix of earthy matcha tones, tropical fruit flavors, and chewy Boba balls. This creation will be a hit at your May the 4th party!

MAKES: 2 DRINKS

4 tablespoons instant tapioca pearl, black sugar flavor

2 kiwis, plus 1 more for garnish (optional)

1 cup pineapple juice

1 teaspoon sweetened matcha powder

8 ounces fizzy water or ginger ale, depending on desired sweetness

1. Prepare the tapioca pearls according to the package directions, and set aside.

2. Peel, core, and roughly chop the kiwis.

3. Combine the pineapple juice, kiwi, and matcha powder in a blender, and blend until smooth.

4. To serve: Fill two large glass tumblers with crushed ice.

5. Split the fruit mixture between the glasses, and ladle half the tapioca pearls into each glass.

6. Top with fizzy water or ginger ale.

7. To garnish, quarter the additional kiwi, cutting a small slit in the center of each quarter. Place two quarters on the rim of each glass, for ears, and, using a short skewer, secure two pearls for eyes.

AHSOKA'S LIGHTSABER NOODLES

WHAT YOU'LL NEED

- 1 green pool noodle
- Craft knife
- Scissors
- Metallic silver duct tape
- Black adhesive vinyl

> **TIP**
>
> You can find pool noodles year-round online.

The weather is finally getting warmer, the twin suns on Tatooine are shining, and the water on Naboo is sparkling. With the kids out of school, this next craft is perfect for the entire family, and you will be able to enjoy these lightsaber pool noodles all year long. I have a special place in my heart for Ahsoka's green lightsabers, but I encourage you to get creative and make lightsabers for different characters and in various colors.

Remember, a Jedi uses the Force for knowledge and defense, never for attack. Beware of where you swing your lightsaber: Don't swing at anyone's head or with intention to harm.

Let's Craft!

1. Using the craft knife, cut a green pool noodle at 1/3 of the length. You should have two pieces, one about 2½ feet long and the other just less than 2 feet long.

2. Use the scissors to cut three pieces of metallic silver duct tape, each about 8 inches long. Wrap the tape horizontally around one pool noodle piece, starting at the bottom edge and overlapping the edges.

3. Cut a piece of black adhesive vinyl about ½ inch wide and 2 inches long. Stick it vertically on the wrapped silver tape, lined up to the top edge.

4. Cut a piece of black adhesive vinyl about ¾ inch wide and 8 inches long. Wrap it around the hilt just above the bottom edge.

5. Cut a small circle from black adhesive vinyl, about ½ inch in diameter. Remove the backing and stick it just below the vertical black strip.

6. Repeat steps 2 through 5 for the other pool noodle piece.

DEATH STAR PIÑATA

Remember the scene in *A New Hope* when Luke Skywalker uses the Force to successfully blow up the Death Star? This iconic moment is followed by a celebration in which our favorite heroes are honored for their life-saving efforts.

I've always wanted to create a Death Star piñata because it's the fun and safe way to destroy the Death Star—and follow it up with a celebration! This is the perfect activity to do at a *Star Wars* party, for kids or adults.

WHAT YOU'LL NEED

- 3 large pieces of cardboard, each at least 12 by 12 inches
- Craft knife
- Ruler
- Hot glue gun
- Candy (any kind)
- Newspaper
- School glue
- Water
- Bowl
- Craft stick
- 20 sheets of metallic silver tissue paper
- Scissors
- Toggle bolt
- Thick string or rope (a few feet in length)

TIPS

- These instructions are for a smaller piñata. To make a bigger one, simply increase the cardboard circle diameter and follow the same steps.
- Be sure to prepare your work surface with more newspaper or another covering when working with papier-mâché.
- Don't forget a stick! Use a piñata stick from a party supply store or a wooden broomstick painted to look like a lightsaber.

Let's Craft!

1. On one piece of cardboard, draw a circle 12 inches in diameter. You can use a large bowl, an empty flowerpot, or another household item as a template.

2. Carefully cut out the circle using the craft knife.

3. On a second piece of cardboard, repeat steps 1 and 2.

4. Cut the third piece of cardboard into five rectangles that are 2 inches wide and 8 inches long.

5. Gently bend each rectangle into a curve. Hot-glue four curved cardboard strips around the perimeter of one cardboard circle. Set aside the last strip.

6. Hot-glue the second cardboard circle on top of the curved edge you just made. Reinforce any gaps in the cardboard with hot glue, as needed.

7. Add the candy to the inside of the piñata. Glue the last strip to the edge, to close the opening.

8. Tear the newspaper into at least fifty thin strips about 6 inches long.

9. Fill the bowl with school glue and water at a ratio of 1:2. Mix gently with the craft stick.

10. Dip a newspaper strip into the glue mixture until it's completely wet. Lay the papier-mâché strip across the 2-inch edge and smooth the ends down on either side.

11. Repeat step 10 until the edges and circles of the piñata are covered in papier-mâché strips. Let the piñata dry, preferably overnight.

12. Using the scissors, cut the silver tissue paper into strips 2 inches

Continued on page 84

tall. Cut the bottom edge of each strip into 1-inch-tall tabs, spaced evenly apart.

13. Glue the strips across one circle side of the piñata, with the metallic side showing, beginning at the bottom. (Make sure the tabs you cut are not glued down.) Keep gluing the strips up the circle until you reach the top.

14. Press and glue down any overlapping tissue paper on the edges of the piñata.

15. Repeat steps 13 and 14 on the other side of the piñata.

16. Using the scissors, cut a circle 4 inches in diameter from the silver tissue paper. Glue the small circle (dull side showing) to the top-left side of one side of the piñata. This is the "dish" of the Death Star.

17. Trim more strips of silver metallic tissue paper 2 inches tall and 2 inches wide. Cut the tabs evenly on the bottom edge.

18. Starting at the bottom of the circle, glue the strips up the right-side edge of the piñata until you reach the top.

19. Repeat step 18 on the left-side edge. Let all the glue dry.

20. Use the craft knife to make a cut about 1 inch long at the top of the piñata. Close the wings of the toggle bolt, and push it through the slit at the top. When released, the wings should lock the bolt in place.

21. Hot-glue the base of the toggle bolt, to secure it.

22. Tie one end of the string to the bolt at the top of the piñata. Throw the other end over a tree branch when it's time to play.

SALACIOUS CRUMB'S BAKE SHOP CUPCAKES

We first meet Salacious Crumb in *Return of the Jedi*: He's the silly jester in Jabba the Hutt's palace. This funny little creature has very little backstory, so I've invented my own fantasy side story for Jabba's tiny but mighty friend. (Note: This story is not *Star Wars* canon—it exists only in my own mind.)

In my imagination, Salacious Crumb loves sweet treats! He sits at Jabba the Hutt's side and devours any little crumb or morsel that falls when Jabba eats. Salacious Crumb dreams of being able to eat whatever he wants one day and fantasizes of eventually breaking away from Jabba and owning his own bake shop. Cupcakes would be his specialty, but he loves all desserts equally. Salacious Crumb definitely has a salty side to his personality, too, so this Salted Caramel Apple Cupcake is sure to be his signature recipe.

MAKES: ABOUT 12 CUPCAKES
SETTING AND COOLING TIME FOR THE CARAMEL: 2 TO 3 HOURS

Caramel Topper:

1½ cups granulated sugar

¼ cup light corn syrup

¼ cup boiling water

¾ cup heavy cream

2 teaspoons vanilla

1 teaspoon kosher salt

Filling:

½ stick or 4 tablespoons butter

½ cup golden brown sugar

1 cup diced apples (about 1 large apple, peeled, cored, and diced)

Cupcakes:

1¾ cups flour, divided

1 teaspoon baking soda

1 teaspoon baking powder

½ teaspoon salt

½ cup unsalted butter, softened to room temperature

½ cup dark brown sugar

¼ cup granulated sugar

2 large eggs, room temperature

½ cup applesauce

1½ cups peeled and chopped apples (about 2 medium apples), tossed with 1 tablespoon fresh lemon juice (set aside)

1 tablespoon vanilla extract

Black lava salt or flake salt, for garnish

Continued on page 84

Special Supplies:

Candy thermometer

Silicone baking mat

🔽 Salacious Crumb Bakeshop logo

1. Have a 10-by-15-inch rimmed baking sheet prepared with a silicone mat or parchment.

2. Let's start with the caramel topper. In a heavy-bottom saucepan with a tight-fitting lid, carefully add the sugar, keeping it as centered in the pan as possible. Add the corn syrup. Pour the boiling water around the edge of the sugar pan, and use a spoon to slowly draw the water through to completely moisten the sugar.

3. Turn the heat to medium, and as soon as the sugar begins to bubble, put on the lid. Leave undisturbed for 5 minutes. When you remove the lid, the sugar should be completely dissolved and clear.

4. Turn up the heat to medium high, and continue to boil the sugar and water mixture without stirring. Periodically check the temperature with a candy thermometer; when the mixture reaches 250°F, heat the heavy cream in the microwave for 1 minute; then leave it until step 5.

5. When the mixture reaches 320°F, remove from heat. Slowly stir in the heavy cream. Be careful and watch for sputtering. Stir continuously until all the cream is incorporated.

6. Return the pan to heat and bring the caramel back up to 250°F. Remove from heat, and stir in the vanilla and salt.

7. Make sure the prepared baking sheet is on a heat-proof surface and in a location it can remain undisturbed. Pour the caramel onto the prepared baking sheet. Tilt the baking sheet, to allow the caramel to spread evenly. Leave to set for 2 to 3 hours.

8. Now let's make the filling. In a skillet that can withstand high heat, melt the butter over medium-high heat.

9. After the butter has melted, scatter the brown sugar over the top of the butter; scatter the apples over the top of that. Let this cook, without stirring, but occasionally shaking the pan, 3 to 5 minutes or until the sugar has dissolved and the apples are tender.

10. Transfer the filling mixture to a heat-proof bowl, and set aside until needed.

11. Finally, let's prepare the cupcakes. Preheat the oven to 425°F. Have a 12-capacity muffin pan lined with cupcake liners.

Continued on page 87

12. Combine 1½ cups flour and the remaining dry cupcake ingredients in a small bowl; set aside.

13. Using a handheld or stand mixer fitted with a paddle attachment, beat the butter and both sugars on high speed until smooth and creamy, about 2 minutes. Scrape down the sides and bottom of the bowl, as needed.

14. Add the eggs and vanilla extract. Beat on medium speed for 1 minute; then turn up to high speed until the mixture is combined and mostly creamy. (It's okay if it appears somewhat curdled.)

15. With the mixer running on low speed, add the dry ingredients and applesauce into the wet ingredients and beat until well combined.

16. Toss the apples with the remaining ¼ cup flour, and fold into the batter.

17. Spoon the batter evenly into each liner, filling each about three-quarters full.

18. Bake 5 minutes at 425°F. Keeping the muffins in the oven, reduce the oven temperature to 350°F. Bake for an additional 15 to 18 minutes or until a toothpick inserted in the center comes out clean.

19. Allow the cupcakes to cool in the pan for 5 minutes before removing them to a wire rack to cool completely.

TO ASSEMBLE THE CUPCAKES:

20. When the cupcakes are completely cool, use a paring knife or a cupcake corer to remove the center of each cupcake (about ½ inch in diameter and 1½ inches deep).

21. Fill each cupcake center with about a tablespoon of apple filling, pressing gently to fill the cavity.

22. Using a 2½-inch-round cookie cutter, cut caramel circles and place one on each cupcake. Stretch gently to cover the whole top. Sprinkle a pinch of flake salt on each cupcake, and serve immediately.

23. Download the Salacious Crumb Bakeshop logo online at www.insighteditions.com/starwarseveryday and use double-sided tape to place them on your cupcake liners.

SALACIOUS CRUMB'S BAKESHOP

A "SPARK"LY GRADUATION CAP

WHAT YOU'LL NEED

- Graduation cap (tassel removed)
- Star stickers
- Hot glue gun
- White glitter alphabet stickers, 1 inch tall
- Glossy glitter scrapbook paper (school color)
- Pencil
- Scissors
- Black glitter alphabet stickers, 1¼ inches tall
- ◆ Rebel Symbol Template (page 16)
- Gold glitter craft foam
- Craft knife

May is an important month for students because it often marks a graduation of some sort. Whether you are a youngling graduating from elementary school, a Padawan graduating from middle or high school, or a Jedi Knight graduating from college, as Obi-Wan would say, "You've taken your first step into a larger world."

During a graduation ceremony, students often look like a sea of clones wearing the same color of robe and hat. However, just like we've learned from the clone troopers, they all have their own personality. One way to express your personality and stick out from the crowd is to decorate the top of your graduation cap. *Star Wars* is full of inspiring quotes to mark a milestone occasion such as a graduation. One of my favorite quotes that comes to mind is, "We are the spark . . . ."

My friend Kelly created an inspiring graduation cap design using this quote and has provided the instructions on the next page. I also recommend getting together a group of graduates for a cap-decorating celebration! Some other *Star Wars* quotes to consider follow:

"This is a new day, a new beginning."

"The Force is strong with this one."

"Try not. Do, or do not. There is no try."

"Never tell me the odds."

"Here's where the fun begins!"

Let's Craft!

1. Rotate the cap so that the front corner is at the top.

2. Place star stickers at every corner of the cap and also centered on the edges between the corner stars. Hot-glue them in place, if needed.

3. Stick additional stars to the top corner of the cap.

4. In white glitter letters, stick **WE** in the center of the cap, just below the stars at the top.

5. In white glitter letters, stick **ARE THE** in the center, just below the **WE**.

6. Draw a starburst shape on the glossy glitter paper, and cut it out using scissors. Make sure the starburst won't cover the tassel button in the center of the cap.

7. In black glitter letters, stick **SPARK** to the starburst shape.

8. Hot-glue the starburst to the bottom of the cap, again being careful not to cover up the tassel button.

9. Download or trace the Rebel Symbol Template (page 16).

10. Flip the gold glitter foam to the nonglitter side. Trace the rebel symbol on the foam, and cut it out with the craft knife.

11. Hot-glue the rebel symbol, glitter side up, to the tassel button. Your cap is complete!

TIPS

- Removing anything that's hot-glued to a graduation cap is difficult, so double-check before you permanently glue something in place!

- Remember, the cap is a diamond shape when worn, not a square.

- You can also download the Rebel Symbol template online at www.insighteditions.com/starwarseveryday.

ADVENTURE

"HERE'S WHERE
THE FUN BEGINS!"

Han Solo, *A New Hope*

MAKE THE KESSEL RUN . . . AT HOME!

Star Wars is full of adventure! One of the most exciting adventures in the *Star Wars* universe is the Kessel Run. For the longest time, we knew very little about this mythical adventure. All we knew was that Han Solo made the Kessel Run in the *Millennium Falcon* in less than 12 parsecs, but every *Star Wars* fan was curious and captivated by what that meant. Thanks to *Solo: A Star Wars Story*, our questions were finally answered, and we got to see Han and his crew complete that famous Kessel Run.

But who says you need to leave home and travel across the galaxy to go on an adventure? For this next activity, I share how you can create your own Kessel Run at home. Use your front yard, back yard, or local park to set up this fun course. Your entire family will have a blast completing this challenge!

WHAT YOU'LL NEED

- 2 cups flour for each person (or pilot) participating (Any type of flour is fine—wheat, rice, coconut, and so on—as long as it's powdered and creates a cloud when thrown into the air.)
- 1 sprinkler or hose
- 1 empty water bottle for every person (or pilot) participating
- Blue food coloring
- 2 large coolers, ice chests, or tubs filled with ice
- 12 large empty cardboard boxes (large enough to stack and create a wall)
- 20 garbage bags filled with crumpled newspaper. (Make sure to use recycled material whenever possible!)
- One large pot with grape tomatoes on the bottom and cooked spaghetti on top
- 1 slip-and-slide, covered in water

First, create your containers of coaxium. To travel at lightspeed, a thin layer of coaxium must line a ship's hyperdrive reaction chamber. Coaxium is mined on the planet Kessel, and smugglers are known to make a Kessel run to avoid Imperial ships. Each person (or pilot) who participates in this Kessel Run challenge must safely deliver a container of your own homemade coaxium at the end of the course. An easy way to create containers of coaxium is to find some empty plastic water bottles, remove the label, fill them three-quarters of the way with water, and add a few drops of blue food coloring. Place these water bottles, or containers of coaxium, at the bottom of a large cooler, ice chest, or tub, and cover the bottles with ice.

Next, plot your course! Create stations and obstacles for your Kessel Run.

1. Pilots should run the course one at a time, beginning with a jump to lightspeed, or a sprint to the next station. This should be a straight line, about 50 feet from the starting line to the next "gas station."

2. Pilots then can "fly" through a channel of gas and water vapor. For the gas station, make sure the cups are full of flour for each pilot. The pilots can throw

TIP

Everyone's space is different, and the distances listed here are just recommendations. You might have to adjust the distance for each station, depending on the amount of space you have to set up the course. Also, all the stations are just recommendations; You can adjust them based on your pilots' mobility. The only rule is to have fun!

Continued on page 94

two cups of flour in the air over their head, one cup at a time, to simulate clouds of ionized gas and fog. (For kids reading this book, make sure you get a parent's permission before participating in this station.)

3. After the gas station, pilots can fly through "water vapor." Set up a sprinkler or hose where water sprays up into the air and comes down like rain. Each pilot can run a circle around the sprinkler ten times.

4. Next, the pilots arrive on Kessel, where they will mine their container of coaxium. The "mine" is the large cooler, ice chest, or tub with water bottles at the bottom. Pilots should search through the ice and grab their container of coaxium.

5. The pilots then have to plow through an Imperial blockade. For this station, set up and stack large empty cardboard boxes to create a wall. Pilots will have to knock down this wall to continue their course.

6. Oh no! A maelstrom! This should be a 25-foot space (or whatever distance your space allows) where pilots can run or zigzag back and forth three times. While the pilots are running, family members or friends will be throwing "asteroids" (trash bags filled with crumpled newspaper) at them. Pilots must try to avoid the asteroids.

7. Now to escape the Maw. At this station, pilots stick their hand into the large pot of cooked spaghetti. The cooked spaghetti

symbolizes the tentacles of the dangerous creature known as the Maw. They need to retrieve a grape tomato from the bottom of the pot, representing a drop of coaxium to give them the extra fuel they need to make the final jump to lightspeed.

8. Now for the final jump to lightspeed! Use the slip-and-slide for this activity; you can buy one from a store, or you can create your own by laying out a large plastic tarp (about 15 feet long) and covering it in water. Pilots will run and slide on their stomach to the end of the slip-and-slide, where they can deliver their container of coaxium and place it in the large container filled with ice.

BALANCE YOUR BODY AND MIND

Not all adventures are fun and exciting, but they still can be rewarding. Some adventures leave us feeling nervous or scared, and these feelings can often present physical symptoms as well. One of the first physical symptoms we notice when we are scared is our heart begins to beat faster. When training to become a Jedi, one must learn how to control their body and their mind.

In *Attack of the Clones*, Jedi Master Obi-Wan Kenobi and his Padawan Anakin Skywalker search for Zam Wesell before she can kill Padmé Amidala. While they are chasing Zam in their cruiser, Anakin suddenly jumps out of their ship, falls several hundred feet, and lands on Zam's ship. A fight ensues and Anakin is angry and scared that he lost his lightsaber in the fight. After catching on fire, Zam's ship crashes causing both her and Anakin to tumble to the ground. The chase continues on foot. Anakin is completely winded from running and angry that he lost Zam Wessel. He had allowed his emotions to spiral out of control. Obi-Wan catches up to Anakin, stops and reminds him to have patience, use the Force, and think. Anakin had to slow down and bring balance back to his body and his mind in order to find Zam Wesell.

In this exercise, you will learn how to bring balance back to your body when stress starts to take over.

1. First, imagine that you are Anakin Skywalker and you are chasing after Zam Wesell. You are running very fast, so inhale and exhale very quickly. If you can run in place, pretend you are sprinting for 15 to 20 seconds, or until you feel your heartbeat increase. If you are not able to run in place, stay seated and move your arms back and forth as you inhale and exhale quickly for 15 to 20 seconds, or until your heartbeat increases.

2. Once you feel your heart pounding, place two fingers on the side of your neck or two fingers on your wrist. You want to be able to feel your heartbeat.

3. Now, slow down your heartbeat with the "One with the Force" Breathing Exercise that can be found on page 12. Connect with the Force as you breathe.

4. Inhale for 4 seconds, hold for 4 seconds, exhale for 4 seconds, and say, "I am one with the Force and the Force is with me." Repeat this as many times as needed until you can feel your heartbeat slow down.

EWOK (BIRD) HOUSE

I have to admit, I love the Ewoks! (Who doesn't?) From the moment I saw Wicket in *Return of the Jedi*, I was hooked! When I was a little girl, I remember having an Ewok plush doll that I carried with me everywhere. I also love the Forest Moon of Endor, with its vibrant green nature and giant redwood trees. My dream as a kid was to have my own Ewok tree house and live out my own *Star Wars* adventure—and to be honest, it's still my dream!

Maybe one day, I'll get to build a full-size tree house, but for this book, I'm excited to share how you can make an Ewok (Bird) House.

Let's Craft!

1. Gather a pile of dry sticks, each about the size and thickness of a pencil.

2. Trim the sticks to the height of the birdhouse walls by either breaking them or cutting with the pruning shears.

3. Hot-glue the sticks around the walls of the birdhouse, making sure to leave the entrance uncovered. Fill in any gaps with small twigs.

4. Hot-glue the wooden coffee stirrers around the roof of the birdhouse. Overlap the stirrers to completely cover the roof.

5. Paint the roof of the birdhouse with the colors you selected. Be creative! Paint it like your favorite *Star Wars* character, use your favorite colors, or leave it natural like the Ewoks' homes.

6. Add any extra decorations to the roof that you'd like, such as rocks and twine.

TIPS

- Craft stores offer wooden birdhouses in various sizes.

- Kids are encouraged to find and break small sticks, but only a grownup should use pruning shears to cut thick sticks to size.

- You can substitute more scavenged sticks if you don't have wooden coffee stirrers.

STAR WARS T-SHIRT BACKPACK

Almost every *Star Wars* character takes some sort of backpack, bag, or pouch when going on an adventure. In it, they carry their snacks, drinks, tools, plans, and companions, among so many other things!

If you're like me, you have a closet or drawer full of old T-shirts—shirts that you love and don't want to get rid of, but ones that you don't necessarily wear anymore. It can be fun to recycle or upcycle old T-shirts and turn them into something new that you'll actually use. One of my favorite crafts to do with an old *Star Wars* T-shirt is turn it into a backpack! This activity is really simple, requires minimal sewing skills, and is fun to do with friends.

WHAT YOU'LL NEED

- T-shirt with a *Star Wars* design on the front
- Scissors
- Sewing pins
- Matching thread
- Needle
- 2 pieces of parachute cord (any color), each at least 5 feet long
- Hot glue gun
- Safety pin

> **TIP**
>
> A size XL T-shirt works best for this activity.

Let's Craft!

1. Flip the T-shirt inside out.

2. Use the scissors to cut off the two sleeves, including the seams, in as straight a line as possible. Save one sleeve piece, and discard the other.

3. Pin the two sleeve holes, and sew them closed. Pin the bottom edge along the hem, and sew it closed.

4. With the scissors, cut the hem from the sleeve piece you saved into two fabric pieces 5 inches long. Fold each piece in half, and pin the ends together to make a loop.

5. Cut a small hole about ½ inch long on one side edge of the T-shirt, about 3 inches from the bottom hem.

6. Slide the pinned T-shirt loop through, folded side first, with the pinned edge sticking out through the hole. Sew it in place.

7. Repeat steps 5 and 6 on the other edge of the T-shirt.

8. Flip the T-shirt through the collar, right side out.

9. Turn over the T-shirt to the back side. Cut two small slits in the top layer of the T-shirt collar fabric, about 4 inches apart. Be careful not to cut all the way through to the bottom layer of the collar.

10. Seal the ends of the two parachute cord pieces with the hot glue gun, to prevent fraying.

11. Affix the safety pin to one end of the parachute cord. Push the safety pin through one slit in the collar.

12. Push the safety pin through the tube you created in the collar until the pin reaches the same slit you started in. Pull the cord through, and remove the safety pin.

13. Thread one end of the pushed-through parachute cord through the bottom loop on the same side of the shirt as the slit you used.

14. Tie the two ends of the parachute cord together, to complete one side of the drawstring strap.

15. Repeat steps 11 through 14 to make the drawstring strap for the other side.

A CLOUD CITY DINNER PARTY

In *The Empire Strikes Back*, Han and Leia must find a safe port to do repairs on the *Millennium Falcon*. Han sees that his old friend Lando Calrissian is reachable on Bespin, and with no other options, they set their course for Cloud City. When the repairs are almost done, Lando takes our heroes to dinner, but they soon find out that it's a trap! The doors open to the dining room, and we see Darth Vader sitting at the head of the dinner table. Lando set up Han and Leia and struck a deal with Vader to turn them in.

   This is a pivotal moment in the movie, and most fans have all sorts of questions: Why would Lando do such a thing? Why did Han and Leia trust Lando? However, I want to know something completely different: What were they going to eat for dinner? As a self-proclaimed foodie, I've always been curious about the dishes served at a Cloud City dinner party. My friend Elena and I brainstormed what Vader might have served, and we came up with a delicious recipe for you to try!

Betrayal with a Side of Rice

MAKES: 8 SERVINGS

Rice:

4 cups water

1 teaspoon kosher salt

1½ cups black forbidden rice

½ cup sweet sticky rice

¼ cup black tahini

6 cloves of black garlic, smashed with the back of your knife for a jamlike consistency

Purée:

16-ounce jar roasted red bell pepper, drained

2 garlic cloves, peeled

One 15-ounce can cannellini beans, drained

½ teaspoon toasted sesame oil

½ teaspoon paprika

1 teaspoon salt

½ teaspoon ginger paste or fresh minced ginger

Black finishing salt (optional)

Tempura Mushroom and Final Plating:

Gluten-free tempura mix, page 102, without the panko

6 ounces enoki or oyster mushrooms, split into small bunches

About 2 quarts neutral frying oil (such as peanut or canola oil)

NOTE: The rice needs to be prepared at least 2 hours ahead.

1. Prepare a 9 x 13 casserole pan by lining it with parchment, allowing some to hang over the ends.

2. Bring 4 cups of water to a boil, add in the salt and black rice. Bring back to a boil and reduce to a simmer.

3. Cover with a tight-fitting lid and cook for 15 minutes. After 15 minutes, add the sweet sticky rice. Bring back to a boil. Cover and simmer for another 15 minutes or until most of the liquid has absorbed.

4. Transfer the rice to a heat proof bowl and stir in the tahini and black garlic until thoroughly incorporated.

5. Spread the rice evenly in the lined pan and chill for at least 1 hour or until needed.

6. For the puree, reserve a ¼ cup of the roasted red pepper. Mince this and set aside for the garnish.

Continued on page 102

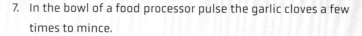

7. In the bowl of a food processor pulse the garlic cloves a few times to mince.

8. Add in the roasted pepper, beans, sesame oil, and spices. Run the food processor until the mixture is a smooth puree, about 1 minutes. Scrape down the sides and pulse a few more times as needed.

9. If using this recipe right away, transfer the puree mixture to a small saucepan and have standing by. If you're making this ahead of time, transfer the mixture to an airtight container and refrigerate until needed.

10. In a large Dutch oven or deep fryer, bring about 2 quarts of oil up to 365°F. Have a cookie sheet lined with a paper towel standing by.

11. While the oil is heating, transfer the purée to a small saucepan and heat over medium heat, stirring occasionally.

12. Preheat the oven to 200°F. Using the parchment, remove the rice from the pan and cut it into 6 equal pieces.

13. When the oil is up to temp, use a metal spatula to lower 1 rice piece at a time into the oil. Allow the rice to cook for 2 to 2½ minutes. Flipping isn't necessary, but gently moving the rice piece while cooking it will help it cook evenly.

14. Using a metal spatula, remove the rice piece, allowing the excess oil to drain off, and transfer it to the paper towel–lined cookie sheet. Repeat with the remaining rice pieces. Transfer the rice pieces to the oven to warm while you prepare the mushrooms.

15. Finish preparing the tempura batter by adding the fizzy water. Line a second cookie sheet with a paper towel. Coat the mushrooms in small batches of 2 or 3 bunches, and add them to the oil. Turn the mushrooms gently while cooking, and remove them when they just start to brown. Gently salt the mushrooms when you remove them from the oil.

16. To assemble: Ladle about ¼ cup purée onto a plate, top with a rice square, top with a mushroom bunch, and scatter some of the reserved red pepper and a few grains of black salt (if you're using it). Serve immediately.

LEIA'S BISCUITS

Before embarking on any adventure, it's wise to pack a snack. You never know whether you'll get stuck somewhere. In *Return of the Jedi*, Leia hops onto a speeder bike to escape some scout troopers in the woods on Endor. Unfortunately, she crash-lands in the forest. An Ewok named Wicket stumbles upon Leia as she lies unconscious on the ground and wakes her up by poking her with his spear. Leia wastes no time in making friends with him. We see Leia open one of the pouches on her belt and take out a cracker, giving it to Wicket as a friendly peace offering. I've always wanted to sample one of Leia's crackers, so Elena and I came up with a recipe that is the perfect snack to pack for your next adventure!

MAKES: ABOUT 3 DOZEN BISCUITS (PICTURED ON PAGE 122)

Dough:

½ cup oats

1 cup unsalted butter, softened

½ cup dark brown sugar

¼ teaspoon salt

2 cups whole-wheat flour

Sugar Coating:

½ cup sugar

1 teaspoon nutmeg

1 teaspoon cinnamon

1. In a medium skillet, over medium-high heat, add the dry oats. Spread them out into an even layer, shaking the pan once or twice to keep them from burning. Let the oats toast for 30 seconds to a minute, or until just fragrant. Transfer them to a plate to cool, and set the plate aside.

2. In the bowl of a stand mixer, or with a hand mixer, beat together the sugar and butter until light and fluffy. Add the salt and flour, and beat until well combined. Add the colled, toasted oats, and stir to combine.

3. Refrigerate for at least 30 minutes. While the dough is refrigerating, mix together all the ingredients for the sugar coating in a small bowl. Preheat the oven to 350°F and prepare 2 cookie sheets with baking mats or parchment.

4. Form balls of dough about 1½ inch in diameter, and roll the balls in the sugar to completely coat them. Place the balls on a prepared cookie sheet. Flatten the dough balls with the bottom of a glass, about 2 inches in diameter. Dip the glass in the sugar after flattening each cookie, to prevent the glass from sticking to the dough.

5. Bake for 10 to 12 minutes or until the cookies are just starting to brown and crisp around the edges.

6. Cool the cookies completely on the cookie sheets; then transfer them to an airtight container. You can store the cookies for 5 days or freeze them for 1 month.

DISCOVERY

"TRULY WONDERFUL
THE MIND OF A CHILD IS."

Jedi Master Yoda, *Attack of the Clones*

CARDBOARD BOX PODRACER

Kids do incredible things in *Star Wars*. Anakin Skywalker, Queen Amidala, and Ahsoka Tano are all children when we first meet them, but they don't let their age define their limits.

This is most certainly the case with young Anakin Skywalker and podracing. Anakin is the only human in the Outer Rim who has the skills to podrace, even at his young age. While on their way to Coruscant for an important mission, Qui-Gon Jinn and Padmé Amidala stop on Tatooine to fix a broken hyperdrive generator. They meet Anakin who suggests that Qui-Gon enter him and the podracer he built in the Boonta Eve Classic so they can then use the prize money for ship repairs. Despite the tremendous amount of pressure, Anakin relishes the opportunity and wins the race, the prize money, and his freedom.

July is the perfect month to play outdoors and this activity is a great way for kids to be creative and active outside; you can even make it a group activity by including your neighbors or friends.

Let's Craft!

1. Using the craft knife, carefully cut the top and bottom flaps from the large cardboard box.

2. Hot-glue two of the flaps to the inside of the back of the box.

3. Cover all top edges of the box with strips of black masking tape.

4. Cut two semicircles about 6 inches in diameter from cardboard or food packaging. Hot-glue them to the inside of the front of the box.

5. Cut a rectangle 5 inches tall from cardboard or food packaging. Cut one side at an angle. Trace the shape on another piece of cardboard to create an identical piece. Hot-glue the pieces on the straight side to the front of podracer. The angled corners should form a V shape toward the center.

6. Decorate the large box with duct tape, plastic lids, bottle caps, and plastic packaging with interesting textures. Set the box aside.

Continued on page 108

WHAT YOU'LL NEED

- Large cardboard box, 18 inches long and 8 inches tall
- Craft knife
- Hot glue gun
- Black masking tape
- Silver duct tape
- Gold duct tape
- Various clean pieces of plastic and food packaging from the recycling bin
- 2 clean 1-liter soda bottles
- 10 sheets of silver tissue paper
- Scissors
- 4 clean toilet paper rolls
- 2 small, clean plastic drink bottles
- Acrylic paint, in various colors
- Markers, in various colors
- Paper hole punch
- String

TIP

- To make this a family activity, parents can put together the podracer and engines and then invite the kids to decorate them.

7. Stuff a 1-liter soft drink bottle with five pieces of rolled-up silver tissue paper. Hot-glue the top of a small plastic drink bottle to the bottom of the 1-liter bottle.

8. Cut cardboard or food packaging into four rectangles 2 inches wide and 6 inches long. Cut the corners on one end of each piece, to make that end rounded.

9. Glue the straight-edged ends of four rectangle shapes around the small drink bottle, printed sides down. These are the engine flaps.

10. Decorate the 1-liter bottle with masking tape and duct tape. Hot-glue small plastic pieces and small cardboard pieces to the bottle, for additional engine parts. Leave the bottom of the bottle undecorated; you'll add something there later.

11. Cut 1-inch-long slits all the way around the end of a toilet paper roll. Hot-glue the uncut side of the roll around the opening of the 1-liter bottle.

12. Repeat steps 7 through 11 with the other 1-liter bottle to make the second engine.

13. It's time to decorate! Paint the pieces with any color of acrylic paint you like, especially for any small cardboard details. Let the paint dry.

14. Use the markers to write letters in Aurebesh, draw *Star Wars* symbols, and create your own designs on the side of the podracer and on the engine flaps.

15. Cut a toilet paper roll lengthwise. Cover the cut edges in masking tape.

16. Punch four holes in the cut corners with the paper hole punch, two on each side.

17. Cut four pieces of string about 4 inches long. Tie one end of each string through each hole you punched.

18. Hot-glue the uncut side of the toilet paper roll to the underside of one 1-liter bottle.

19. Repeat steps 15 through 18 with the other toilet paper roll and 1-liter bottle.

20. To make a strap, cut a piece of duct tape about 2 feet long. Lay it on a table with the non-sticky side down.

21. Cut a piece of duct tape about 1½ feet long. Stick it to the center of the duct tape piece on the table, sticky side to sticky side. The ends of the tape should still be sticky.

22. Stick the strap to the left side of the podracer box on the inside, with one end near the seat and the other close to the front. Tape down the ends with additional pieces of duct tape, for a durable hold.

23. Repeat steps 20 through 22 to make a strap for the right side, and your podracer is complete.

DISCOVERING DIPLOMACY

As the ruler of Naboo, Queen Amidala had to learn diplomacy at a young age. In *Star Wars: The Clone Wars*, we learn that she was only 14 when she was elected queen, yet she was identified as one of Naboo's most intelligent and brightest minds. Queen Amidala was committed to her people and to freedom and democracy.

I was a teenage girl when *The Phantom Menace* came out, and I was in awe of Queen Amidala. I had never seen a girl so close to my own age involved in politics. On Naboo, young women were often elected because they offered a pure, childlike wisdom and care that most adults no longer possessed.

Diplomacy can simply be described as the skill of dealing with people effectively in a positive way. I've listed some conversation starters you can share with any children in your life, to encourage diplomatic conversations. To use *Star Wars* as an example, imagine that the classroom is the Galactic Senate and the child is Queen Amidala.

1. Imagine that your classmates have picked you as their class leader. In this role, you represent the entire class and their wishes to the principal. What does it mean to you to be the class leader?

2. How do you know what questions your classmates have for the principal, and how can you make sure you represent your entire class?

3. What if your class disagrees on something? Imagine that you can together pick only one elective. Some students want to pick an art class; other students want to pick a music class. You are the one who must go to the principal and pick the class. How do you decide on an answer? Are you able to make the entire class happy?

4. How can you keep peace in the class when some students are unhappy with the choice you made?

5. What's one thing you can do to bring your class together and make everyone happy?

HOTH-SICLES

When it feels like Tatooine outside, eating something as cold as Hoth is exactly what we crave! I have fond memories of making homemade ice pops with my mom when I was younger. Frozen treats are a staple in the summer, and these Hoth-sicles are easy for kids to make with parental supervision.

The next time the kids (and adults, too!) are hot and hungry, have some of these Hoth-sicles ready to go in the freezer. They make the perfect afternoon snack for warm summer days.

MAKES: 12 HOTH-SICLES

3 cups coconut water, divided

2 envelopes (about 5 teaspoons) unflavored gelatin

2 tablespoons butterfly pea flower

½ cup cane sugar, divided

One 13-ounce can coconut milk

1 teaspoon vanilla paste

Special Supplies:

Silicone ice mold

Popsicle mold

1. Place ½ cup coconut water in a small bowl, and sprinkle in the gelatin, allowing it to stand for 5 minutes and bloom.

2. Combine 1½ cups coconut water, butterfly pea flower, and ¼ cup of the cane sugar in a small saucepan. Bring to a boil. When the mixture is boiling and the sugar has dissolved, remove the pan from heat and strain it into a bowl. Add the bloomed gelatin and stir until the gelatin is melted.

3. Pour the mixture into a silicone ice mold with small cavities (I used a 1-inch hexagon shape), and freeze for at least 1 hour.

4. When the gelatin has been in the freezer for at least an hour, you can start making the coconut milk mixture. Combine the reserved 1 cup coconut water, remaining cane sugar, vanilla paste, and coconut milk. Stir until the sugar dissolves.

5. Have your popsicle molds ready. Place the coconut water gelatin pieces in each mold, either as is or torn to create jagged shapes. Fill each mold about a third of the way full of gelatin pieces.

6. Pour the coconut milk mixture to the fill line of each mold. Use a chopstick or long spoon to gently move the gelatin pieces, allowing the coconut milk to flow around them. Top off as necessary.

7. Freeze for 4 hours or until firm. Unmold and serve immediately.

GROGU PAPER BAG PUPPET

WHAT YOU'LL NEED

- Ruler
- Pencil
- Lime green cardstock or construction paper
- Pink cardstock or construction paper
- Black cardstock or construction paper
- Blue cardstock or construction paper
- White cardstock or construction paper
- Cream cardstock or construction paper
- Scissors
- Brown paper lunch bag
- School glue
- ⬇ Grogu Paper Bag Puppet template
- Paper hole punch
- Dark blue marker

If you're a *Star Wars* fan, it's now impossible to hear the words *the child* and not think of Grogu. He has arguably become the most iconic child in *Star Wars*. Even kids who haven't seen *The Mandalorian* know who Grogu is, and the obsession with this adorable character has become a global phenomenon.

I'm always looking for easy arts and crafts to do with my nieces and nephews, so I came up with the idea to make a Grogu paper bag puppet when I was babysitting my 5-year-old nephew. He absolutely loved this simple but fun craft, and I'm sure you will, too!

Let's Craft!

1. Use the ruler and pencil to measure a rectangle on the bright green paper that is 4½ inches long by 2 inches wide (or the same size as the bottom of the lunch bag). Cut out the rectangle with scissors.

2. Glue the green paper to the bottom of the lunch bag, to make Grogu's face.

3. Download the ear shape from the puppet template at www.insighteditions.com/starwarseveryday. Trace the ear twice on the green paper, and cut out the two ears.

4. Cut out two thin teardrop shapes from the pink paper, for the inside of Grogu's ears. Glue them next to the short, straight edge of the ears.

5. Glue the ears to the paper bag in the folded space behind the face, with the straight edge at the top and the pink pieces facing forward.

6. Trace the eye shape twice on the black paper, and cut these out to make Grogu's eyes. Glue them on the face.

7. Use the paper hole punch to make two small holes in the white paper. Glue one on each eye as reflections.

8. Cut a small half-circle from the green paper and glue it between Grogu's eyes. (This is his little nose.)

9. Cut a piece of black paper 4 inches long by 2 inches wide. Fold it in half lengthwise.

10. Make two small cuts about a centimeter apart in the center of the fold. Partially unfold the paper and gently push the cut paper through to make a tab.

11. Fold the paper in half again, with the tab on the inside. Glue it to the inside flap under the face. Make sure the tab opens out at a 90-degree angle when the mouth opens.

12. Trace the frog template on the blue paper and cut it out. Add stripes to the frog's legs with the blue marker.

13. Glue the frog to the bottom part of the tab inside the mouth.

14. Cut a piece of the cream paper 6 inches long and 2 inches wide. Cut it in half vertically.

15. Overlap and glue the cream-colored pieces on the bag below Grogu's head, to make the top of his robe.

TIPS

- Don't use too much glue inside Grogu's mouth, or it might stay closed!

- You can skip the template and easily freehand all pieces, if needed.

PLANET PAPER LANTERNS

WHAT YOU'LL NEED

- 3 white paper lanterns, in various sizes
- Newspaper
- White glitter
- School glue
- Light blue acrylic paint
- Small spray bottle
- Water
- Light green acrylic paint
- Paintbrush
- Red acrylic paint
- Orange acrylic paint
- Black acrylic paint
- 3 small *Star Wars* toy vehicles, such as an X-wing, a TIE fighter, or a snowspeeder
- Three 10-milimeter closed jump rings
- Hot glue gun
- White string

TIPS

- Mustafar is a small planet, so you can choose the smallest lantern for it.
- Use other colors in the paint mixes for different planets. You might use brown and forest green for Dagobah, tan for Jakku or Tatooine, and orange for Bespin. You can also team up with your family to make your own colorful *Star Wars*–inspired planets.
- Place a battery-powered tea light inside the lantern to add a soft glow.

I've always been fascinated by the variety of planets in the *Star Wars* galaxy. Each planet has its own unique atmosphere, habitat, and terrain. From the frigid climate of Hoth, to the tropical climate of Scarif, to the molten planet of Mustafar, we can learn so much planetary science from *Star Wars*.

Even though it's summer and most kids are out of school, learning about the planets in *Star Wars* is a great way to continue kids' education during this time of year. This activity is all about discovery and learning in a way that doesn't feel like homework. Use these *Star Wars* planets as a jumping off point to talk about our own solar system. We've chosen Hoth, Scarif, and Mustafar for this activity, but you can challenge your Padawans to study all the *Star Wars* planets and pick their top three.

Let's Craft!

1. Assemble the three paper lanterns according to the accompanying instructions. Prepare your work surface by laying out newspaper.

2. Choose one lantern for the icy planet of Hoth.

3. Spread a thin layer of school glue across one section of the lantern. Sprinkle the white glitter to cover it. Let the lantern dry.

4. Shake off the excess glitter. Then move on to the next section of the lantern with another layer of glue and glitter.

5. Repeat step 3 until the white paper lantern is completely covered in glitter "snow."

6. Gather the excess glitter on the newspaper, and return it to the container to save it for a future craft. Set aside the Hoth lantern.

7. Choose a lantern for the watery planet of Scarif.

8. Fill the small spray bottle about a third full of the light blue acrylic paint. Fill the remaining space with water, and shake well to mix.

9. Spray the paper lantern with the light blue paint mix until it is completely covered. Clean out the spray bottle, and let the lantern dry.

10. Use the paintbrush and light green acrylic paint to add small

islands around the blue paper
lantern. Let all the paint dry, and
set aside the Scarif lantern.

11. The remaining paper lantern is
for the volcanic planet Mustafar.
Fill the small spray bottle about a
third full of the red acrylic paint.
Fill the remaining space with
water, and shake well to mix.

12. Spray the paper lantern with
the red paint mix until it is
completely covered. Let the
lantern dry.

13. Use the paintbrush and orange
acrylic paint to add more lava to
the red paper lantern.

14. Lightly dry brush black acrylic
paint across the surface, for more
lava. Let all the paint dry.

15. Hot-glue one jump ring to the
top of each *Star Wars* vehicle.

16. Tie one vehicle to each lantern
with a piece of string a few inches
long. For example, the X-wing can
fly below Scarif, the TIE fighter

can fly below Mustafar, and the
snowspeeder can fly below Hoth.

17. Tie another piece of string a few
inches long to the top of each
paper lantern. Experiment with
different lengths of strings when
you hang the lanterns from the
ceiling.

STAR WARS SLUSHIES

When you visit the planet of Batuu at *Star Wars* Galaxy's Edge while at a Disney Park, it's often very hot, humid, and muggy. One of my favorite things to do is stop by the milk stand and get a cool and refreshing glass of frozen blue or green milk.

When I was a young girl growing up in Florida during the hot summers, I set up a drink stand in my front yard and sold various homemade drinks to my neighbors. Not only was this a great way for me to explore new recipes, but it also taught me how to run a small business. If I set up my drink stand now, I would definitely serve these two *Star Wars*–inspired shaved ices. The entire neighborhood would be calling for these drinks during the hot summer!

MAKES: ABOUT 6 DRINKS

1 recipe of either Yoda Punch, page 77 or Tatooine Purple Juice, page 70

Special Supplies:

9-by-13-inch baking dish (glass works best)

1. Pour the punch or juice into the baking dish, and place the dish flat in the freezer. (There's no need to cover it.) After 1 hour, scrape the mixture with a fork, pulling the ice crystals from the bottom and the sides.

2. Continue to freeze the mixture for a total of 3 hours, scraping it with a fork every 30 to 45 minutes.

3. When all the liquid has formed into ice crystals, the shaved ice is ready. Transfer it to an airtight container and put it in the freezer until you're ready to use it.

4. To serve: You can enjoy the shaved ice as is, serve it with a scoop of ice cream, or combine it with soda. No shaved ice machine needed!

SAND . . . BUT MAKE IT FUN!

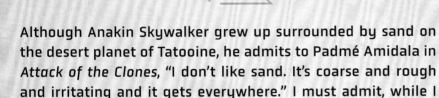

Although Anakin Skywalker grew up surrounded by sand on the desert planet of Tatooine, he admits to Padmé Amidala in *Attack of the Clones*, "I don't like sand. It's coarse and rough and irritating and it gets everywhere." I must admit, while I absolutely love going to the beach, I'm not the biggest fan of sand—it truly *does* get everywhere!

However, when it comes to sand, there are many benefits, too. While every child is different, playing with sand can be a great sensory exercise for some kids. Sensory play supports brain development in kids and stimulates the senses. Playing with sand can also be very calming and reduces stress for both kids and adults.

A great way to play with sand without having to make a trip to the beach is to make it at home. The following recipe for homemade kinetic sand is easy, and kids will love discovering all the things they can create with it. This recipe is safe for little mouths if they happen to taste it, but this is not food, so please do not eat it.

WHAT YOU'LL NEED

- 1 cup baking soda
- ½ cup sugar
- ½ cup corn starch
- 1 tbsp cream of tartar
- ¼ cup water
- Food coloring, color of your choice

1. Start by mixing the dry ingredients in a bowl.

2. Mix your food coloring and water in another bowl.

3. Gradually add your colored water mixture, 1 tbsp at a time, to your dry ingredients and mix well. Your mixture will have a sand-like texture but will be damp enough to mold. Have fun!

TIP

Once you've created your kinetic sand, have unstructured play time for the whole family. Build and create *Star Wars* characters, ships, and symbols. The following recipe creates one single batch, so I recommend making several batches in different colors if you want various sand creations.

POWER

"POWER! UNLIMITED POWER!"

Darth Sidious, *Star Wars: Episode III Revenge of the Sith*

SHARE THE FORCE

Power is a very important theme in *Star Wars*. Oftentimes, when people think of power, they think of something that is shown or taken with physical force. However, the strongest powers in *Star Wars* are not physical at all. Power is shown through love, kindness, selflessness, knowledge, inspiration, and hope.

A spark of hope can bring down an Empire, the love between a father and son can destroy the dark side, and a selfless act can save the Resistance. One of the biggest lessons I learned from being the voice of Ahsoka Tano is that kindness is powerful. When Ahsoka walked away from the Jedi Order at the end of season 5 in *Star Wars: The Clone Wars*, she was lost. She had lost her home, her identity, her purpose, everything.

Not knowing where she was going or what she was doing, she stumbled upon two sisters, Trace and Rafa Martez, who were in trouble and needed her help. Without question, Ahsoka joined the sisters on a dangerous mission and helped get them home safely. After this mission, Ahsoka discovered that her purpose is to help people. She went on to be one of the founders of the Rebellion and she continued to spread hope, light, and kindness across the galaxy.

This next exercise is a pay-it-forward practice of kindness I call "Share the Force." It's simple, but so rewarding.

1. Make your kindness notes. Get red or orange paper, and trace and cut out multiple rebel symbols by using the template on page 16. Glue the symbols on a small note card and write the message, "You are the chosen one for this act of kindness. Always remember that the Force is strong with you. Please keep this flow of energy going and share the Force with someone else."

2. Now, share the Force! Take your kindness cards with you and find an act of kindness that you can do. Your act of kindness can be simple, like holding the door open for someone, giving someone a compliment, or helping someone carry something when their hands are full. Give one of your cards to the recipient of your act of kindness.

3. Repeat steps 1 and 2 often. Make kindness a part of your daily routine.

TIP

You can also download and print as many rebel symbols as you would like at www.insighteditions.com/starwarseveryday.

KNOWLEDGE IS POWER

We often hear the phrase, "Knowledge is power." In the *Star Wars* galaxy, knowledge is definitely a powerful asset. In *The Empire Strikes Back*, Jedi Master Yoda teaches Luke Skywalker, "A Jedi uses the Force for knowledge and defense, never for attack."

However, the dark side uses knowledge as a weapon: Chancellor Palpatine turns Anakin Skywalker to the dark side in *Revenge of the Sith* when he says, "Learn to know the dark side of the Force and you will be able to save your wife from certain death . . . . Use my knowledge, I beg you." How you use the knowledge you seek is up to you. It's your path, and you must decide.

This next activity puts your knowledge to the test! I love playing *Star Wars* trivia with friends and family. By following these instructions, you can make *Star Wars* trivia cards for your next game night . . . and use your knowledge for good!

WHAT YOU'LL NEED

- 🔽 Trivia card template
- 🔽 Trivia questions template
- Scissors
- Ruler
- Pencil
- Cardstock or construction paper, in various colors
- School glue

TIP

Make extra cards with one blank side, and ask your friends and family members to write in their own questions and answers. Can they stump you?

Let's Craft!

1. Download, print, and cut out twenty-one cards from the trivia card template from www.insighteditions.com/starwarseveryday.

2. Then download, print, and cut out the twenty-one questions from the trivia questions template, located online as well.

3. Cut the various colors of paper into twenty-one rectangles 4 inches long by 3 inches wide.

4. Glue the card front to one side of the rectangle, and glue the question to the other. Repeat this for all trivia questions.

JEDI TRAINING SNACK BOX

When Luke Skywalker goes to Dagobah to find Jedi Master Yoda, he sets up camp after his X-wing crashes into the swamp. Hungry after a long trip, he pulls out a rations kit, or a snack box, to eat. We don't get a good look at what's inside this bento-like box, but it was clearly full of snacks to give Luke fuel for his training.

We do see Luke pull out a snack bar of some sort and take a bite. I imagine that this is some sort of *Star Wars* protein bar. I'm a big fan of protein bars, and I often have one in my bag when I'm out for a long day and don't have time to sit down for a meal. I was so excited to work with Elena to create a recipe for a *Star Wars*–inspired protein bar like the one in Luke's rations kit.

Jedi Padawan Protein Pods

MAKES: ABOUT 12 BARS

1 cup rolled oats

½ cup raw almonds

½ cup raw pumpkin seeds

½ cup raw sunflower seeds

½ cup unsweetened coconut flakes

2 tablespoons chia seeds

¼ teaspoon salt

½ cup chopped apricot

2 tablespoons nut or seed butter of choice

2 tablespoons melted coconut oil

¼ cup maple syrup

> **TIP**
>
> Fill the rest of your snack box with healthy snacks that will provide energy and fuel for training. Some suggestions:
> • Leia's Biscuits, page 103
> • Rey's Portion Bread, page 46
> • Pretzels
> • Carrot sticks
> • Beef jerky
> • Dried fruit leather

1. Preheat the oven to 350°F, and prepare an 8-by-8-inch pan with parchment. (Allow the parchment to overhang the edges of the pan.)

2. On a rimmed baking sheet, combine the oats, almonds, pumpkin seeds, and sunflower seeds. Toast for 10 to 12 minutes or until fragrant but not browning.

3. In a large bowl, combine the coconut flakes, chia seeds, salt, and chopped apricot. Set aside.

4. When the nuts and seeds are toasted, add them to the bowl and stir to combine. Reduce the oven temp to 325°F.

5. In a small saucepan over medium heat, combine the nut butter, coconut oil, and maple syrup. Stir until well combined, and bring to a simmer. Remove from heat and add to the bowl. Stir well to make sure the whole mixture is evenly coated.

6. Pour the mixture into the prepared pan, and press it into an even layer. Bake for 20 to 25 minutes or until the edges are just starting to brown. Allow the mixture to cool completely.

7. Use the parchment to lift the mixture out of the pan, and slice it into 12 bars. Store the bars in an airtight container, with parchment between the layers.

MAZ KANATA'S FRUIT CUPS

In *The Force Awakens*, Han, Rey, Finn, and BB-8 travel to Takodana to visit Maz Kanata and seek information on how to get BB-8 back to the Resistance. When they enter Maz's castle, they walk into a party already in progress. A live band is performing, games are being played, and all sorts of food and drinks are being served. When they sit down with Maz, we see a giant bowl of exotic-looking fruits in the center of the table. Hungry from a long journey, Rey eats something that looks like half an apple filled with other interesting items.

Whatever she's eating looks healthy and refreshing, the perfect power snack to keep her fueled for her mission. Although I'm not quite sure what's in the middle of the fruit cup, Elena and I put made our best guess to bring you this recipe. The next time you're on the hunt for a powerful snack to bring you energy, this is the one you're looking for!

MAKES: 2 FRUIT CUPS

2 medium apples

1 tablespoon apple cider vinegar

¼ cup seed butter

2 tablespoons honey

About ½ cup blueberries

4 slices dried or freeze-dried kiwi

Special Supplies:

Melon baller

1. Cut each apple in half, from top to bottom. Cut and slice two of the apple halves, tossing the slices in a bowl with the apple cider vinegar.

2. With the other two apple halves, use a melon baller to gently carve out the interior and remove the core. Discard the seeds and bits of core. Add the apple pieces to the bowl, and toss them to coat. Set aside the apple pieces.

3. In a small bowl, combine the seed butter with the honey, and stir until smooth. Split the mixture between the two apple bowls, and top it with blueberries, apple pieces, and kiwi. Serve immediately.

MAKE YOUR OWN (NO-SEW) JEDI ROBE

WHAT YOU'LL NEED

- 2 brown XL T-shirts
- Scissors
- Masking tape
- ⬇ Hood pattern (optional)
- Sewing pins
- Hot glue gun

Every Jedi Padawan needs a robe—it's a staple in any Jedi wardrobe. Whether they need to conceal their identity or just cover up from the elements, a Jedi robe makes a powerful fashion statement.

This next activity is so much fun to create with kids! They can help make their own Jedi robe to wear as they train to be Jedi, whether individually or as part of a Jedi Training Party (page 63).

This activity doesn't require sewing, but we do recommend using a hot glue gun, so adult supervision is needed. Follow the instructions to make the perfect Padawan-size Jedi robe.

Let's Craft!

1. Stick a small piece of masking tape a few inches long on the collar of one T-shirt so that the edge of the tape marks the center of the shirt.

2. Keep sticking on small pieces, lined up down the center, to mark the middle line of the T-shirt.

3. Cut only the front of the shirt (the top layer) down the center, using the tape as a guide.

4. Remove the tape, and set aside the robe.

5. Download, print, and cut out the hood pattern from www.insighteditions.com/ starwarseveryday. Pin the hood pattern on the bottom of the other brown T-shirt, lining up the straight edge of the pattern with the bottom hem.

6. Cut out the hood with scissors, through both the front and the back, to make two pieces. If you'd like a bigger hood, skip using the pattern and cut a similar shape from the entire bottom half of the T-shirt.

7. Either save the rest of the T-shirt for scrap fabric or discard it.

8. Pin the two hood pieces with the right sides together. The nicer bottom hems, which will frame the face, should be on the inside.

9. Remove the pins as you hot-glue the top curved edge of the hood together on the inside. Proceed carefully so you don't burn your fingers—the fabric will be hot!

10. Flip the hood right side out, and flatten the shape so that the seam is in the center.

11. Hot-glue the outside bottom edge of the hood to the inside of the robe collar.

TIPS

- The template and instructions are intended for making kid-size robes.

- If you're in a hurry or you have a lot of robes to make, you can skip the hood and use just one shirt as a loose Jedi robe.

LIGHTSABER TRAINING EXERCISE

In *Attack of the Clones*, Anakin Skywalker loses his lightsaber while trying to catch Zam Wesell in a high-speed chase. Luckily for Anakin, his Jedi Master, Obi-Wan Kenobi, finds his lightsaber and delivers it back to him with the reminder, "Next time, try not to lose it . . . . This weapon is your life." A Jedi uses this very powerful weapon to protect others. Jedi carefully train to use their lightsabers for protection, never for malice.

During their time at the Jedi Temple, Padawans train extensively with their lightsabers. Successfully using a lightsaber is part skill and part feel. When Jedi Master Yoda trains younglings to use their lightsabers in *Attack of the Clones*, he advises, "Reach out, sense the Force around you. Use your feelings you must." You must be one with the Force to sense where an attack is coming from. This is a skill that can be honed only with practice!

Grab your family and friends for a fun and powerful lightsaber training exercise.

1. To get started, make sure everyone has space to move.

2. At the same time, everyone should throw their balloons up into the air. The goal is to keep your balloons in the air with your lightsaber and stop them from touching the ground.

3. As the balloons fly around the room, work together as a team to keep them from hitting the floor.

4. Of course, having multiple balloons in the air makes it hard to keep an eye on all of them at the same time. This is where you must use the Force and sense where to swing your saber to keep the balloons floating. Be mindful of your surroundings—your lightsabers should swing only at balloons, not at other people.

PATIENCE

"PATIENCE YOU MUST HAVE,
MY YOUNG PADAWAN."

Jedi Master Yoda, *The Empire Strikes Back*

PATIENCE PADA

LEARN AUREBESH

To write in Aurebesh, the name for the alphabet used in *Star Wars*, you'll need to practice being patient. Learning another language can be difficult and time consuming. I've always wanted to learn Aurebesh, but to be honest, I've never had the patience to sit down and do it . . . until now! Then my friend Kelly came up with a brilliant craft to make for this exercise: an Aurebesh decoder. This decoder makes learning to read and write in this mysterious *Star Wars* language much easier.

A great way to practice is to write someone a letter in Aurebesh. You can even follow the "Reach Out" exercise on page 61 and send a friend or family member a letter in Aurebesh using your decoder.

You can even follow the "Reach Out" exercise on page 61

WHAT YOU'LL NEED

- ⬇ Aurebesh Decoder template
- White cardstock
- Scissors
- Cardboard food packaging
- Math compass
- Pencil
- Cardboard and plastic pieces from the recycling bin
- 7 small googly eyes
- School glue
- Gold acrylic paint
- Silver acrylic paint
- Black acrylic paint
- Paintbrush
- String
- Paper brad
- Dot stickers

Let's Craft!

1. Print out the Aurebesh decoder template from www.insighteditions.com/starwarseveryday on white cardstock, and cut out the template with the scissors.

2. On a clean piece of cardboard food packaging, draw a circle 4 inches in diameter; cut it out.

3. Cut out a small square on the edge of the cardboard circle, about ¼ inch by ¼ inch.

4. Press the tip of your pencil into the center of the cardboard circle, to make a hole where you will later place the paper brad.

5. Glue the small googly eyes around the edge of the circle.

6. Cut small rectangular pieces of cardboard and plastic packaging in various sizes—the more interesting textures you can find, the better!

7. Glue the small packaging pieces to the cardboard circle, to mimic various mechanisms. Be sure to leave room for the paper brad in the center. Let the glue dry.

8. Paint the entire circle and all the glued pieces with the gold acrylic paint, and let the paint dry.

9. Dry brush black paint to add "dirt," and add silver paint on the edges of all pieces to add weathering.

10. Glue a piece of string between some of the pieces, to act as a wire.

11. Push the paper brad through the center of the top circle and then again through the center of the cardstock decoder. Make sure the alphabet letters are clearly visible beneath the circle you painted.

12. Push down the prongs in the back.

13. Add other details, such as dot stickers, to finish the decoder.

TIPS

- If you're putting together more than one decoder, make a template for the inner circle.

- Little bits and bobs that add details to make an item feel like it belongs in *Star Wars* by Matthew Stover are called greebles, or greeblies. Almost anything in your recycling bin can turn into a good greeblie!

MEDITATION . . . PRACTICE YOU MUST

In *Star Wars: The Clone Wars*, in an episode called "Assassin," Ahsoka Tano experiences troubling dreams and visions, which she believed were telling her that something bad was going to happen to someone close to her. Jedi Master Yoda confirmed her suspicions and told her she was having premonitions. He advised that this is the true power of the Force, and she should not underestimate her visions. However, in order to better understand what her premonitions were telling her, she must meditate. Master Yoda says, "Meditate to see clearly, more experience you need." Meditation is a skill that needs regular practice and dedication.

It can be difficult for something to become a regular part of your routine if you do not create a space and time for it in your day. A great way to help you stick to a regular meditation practice as a part of your routine is to create a dedicated meditation space. The following tips will help you create your own meditation space, so you can practice and create a habit.

1. Find a calming space where there are few distractions; a quiet space where you feel comfortable. This should be a place that brings you joy or a space that is neutral when it comes to your emotions. Also ensure this space has enough room for you to lie down. If you do not have access to a quiet, calming space, get creative. Sometimes, just going into the bathroom, a pantry, or closet and shutting the door for a few minutes of privacy may be your only option. Look for a place where you won't be interrupted, and you'll have a moment of privacy.

2. Surround yourself with anything that makes you happy, such as calming music or a speaker, a water fountain or a white noise machine, or plants and other greenery. It's your space, so make it calming to you.

3. If you are someone who finds peace and calm outside, find a spot that you can safely and regularly go to. Being outdoors and in nature can be very peaceful.

Fulcrum Yoga Mat

The ideal meditation space is going to look different for everyone. What's most important is how you feel in this space. This should be a space that you want to visit often for moments of peace, quiet, calm, and mindfulness. Sometimes, I prefer to sit, but other times I prefer to lie down. And I always have a yoga mat ready to lie on in my meditation space.

As one of the founders of the Rebellion in *Star Wars Rebels*, Ahsoka Tano had to keep her identity hidden for safety, so she used the Fulcrum symbol as a secret identity for the *Ghost* crew. She later revealed herself as Fulcrum, and to *Star Wars* fans, it has become a symbol of hope. One way you can incorporate this symbol into your every day is to make your own Fulcrum symbol yoga mat. Follow the instructions below to paint your own mat to help elevate your mediation space.

Let's Craft!

1. Trace the Fulcrum template on the left on cardstock paper or download it online at www.insighteditions.com/starwarseveryday.

2. Carefully cut out the symbol from the paper with the craft knife. Discard the pieces you cut out.

3. Place the template sheet on the yoga mat so that the top and left edges of the paper line up with the top and left edges of the mat. Tape the template in place.

4. Place newspaper or a drop cloth around the template to catch overspray.

5. In a well-ventilated area, spray the template with the white fabric spray paint. Wait a few minutes before removing the template.

6. Give the paint more time to dry per the directions on the bottle.

7. Next, place the template sheet on the yoga mat so that the top and right edges of the paper line up with the top and right edges of the mat.

8. Repeat steps 4 though 6.

9. Place the template in the center between the two symbols you've already painted.

10. Repeat steps 4 though 6.

11. Once all paint is dry, repeat steps 3 through 10 on the other end of the mat.

- ⊙ Fulcrum template, below
- Cardstock paper
- Craft knife
- 1 yoga mat (solid color)
- Masking tape
- Newspaper or drop cloth
- White fabric spray paint

FULCRUM TEMPLATE

EXPLORE THE FORCE

There is a lot of talk in *Star Wars* about the Force, but what *exactly is* the Force? Jedi Master Yoda teaches Luke Skywalker in *The Empire Strikes Back*, "My ally is the Force and a powerful ally it is. Life creates its, makes it grow. Its energy surrounds us and binds us. Luminous beings are we, not this crude matter. You must feel the Force around you." Years later, and once Luke Skywalker became a Jedi Master himself, he passes on the knowledge to Rey in *The Last Jedi*, "The Force is not a power you have. It's not about lifting rocks. It's the energy between all things, a tension, a balance, that binds the universe together."

To become one with the Force, you must connect with your surroundings. The following is a quick grounding exercise that you can do to connect or reconnect with the Force, especially when you are feeling stressed or like things are moving too fast or out of control. It's also a great way to calm your mind and practice patience.

To get started, visit your meditation space (page 135), and sit in a comfortable position. If you are not at home or don't have your meditation space ready, find a safe place where you can sit down for a few minutes. Next, count down from 5 as you follow the prompts below.

5: Say 5 things that you can see around you.

4: Touch 4 things that you feel around you.

3: Listen to 3 things than you can hear around you.

2: Notice 2 things that you can smell around you.

1: Identify one thing that you can taste. If you can't taste anything in that moment, name a taste that you like.

> **TIP**
>
> Repeat this grounding exercise whenever you feel stressed, nervous, or like you need to slow down the moment and become one with your surroundings.

PATIENCE IN THE KITCHEN

When I was younger, I didn't have the patience for cooking, so I wanted to cook only recipes that were easy and quick. On one occasion, my Italian grandmother and I spent all day in the kitchen cooking her spaghetti sauce and meatballs, and I never understood how she had the patience to cook that long. As I got older, I realized that cooking in the kitchen was a good way for me to practice patience myself. I've had many successes and also many failures in the kitchen, but after years of cooking, I've found my patience and have really grown to love cooking. As we practice patience this month, the following recipes will be perfect for the start of the colder season. Both recipes are inspired by Luke Skywalker and his time on Ahch-To.

Luke Skywalker's Fish Bake

In *The Last Jedi*, Luke's food source was limited to what was available on the island. He had to catch his own fish, a practice that also takes a tremendous amount of patience. We don't actually see how he cooks the giant fish he catches, but with only a fire to cook over, he probably would have done some sort of fish bake. After a bit of research, Elena came up with this delicious recipe for Luke Skywalker's Fish Bake.

MAKES: 4 SERVINGS

2 pounds sweet potatoes (purple, if available)

2 cups vegetable broth

One 13-ounce can light coconut milk

2 tablespoons Thai green curry paste

1 red bell pepper, seeded and sliced

1½ pounds Atlantic cod

1 tablespoon lemongrass paste

4 green onions, white and light green parts, sliced

Cooked rice (optional)

1. Peel and slice the sweet potatoes about ¼ inch thick. If the slices get too large, cut them into half-moons.

2. In a medium saucepan, combine the broth, coconut milk, and curry paste, and bring the mixture to a low boil. Reduce to a simmer and add the purple sweet potatoes. Simmer for 5 minutes, and then add the red bell pepper. Simmer for another 7 to 10 minutes or until the vegetables are tender.

3. While the vegetables are simmering, heat the broiler to high. On a foil-lined baking sheet, smear the lemongrass paste evenly over all the pieces of cod. Broil for 3 to 5 minutes, watching carefully, until the fish is flaky and starting to brown.

4. To serve: Ladle the vegetables and the sauce into the bottom of a shallow bowl (over rice, if using), and place a piece of fish on top. Scatter sliced green onions over the fish.

Not Porg Squash Roast

In *The Last Jedi*, Chewbacca has limited food options on Ahch-To and plans a dinner of roast porg. However, he has an audience of several porgs staring at him with their big, sad eyes. Feeling the pressure, Chewbacca never actually eats the roast porg.

   In lieu of a porg roast, we wanted to imagine a plant-based option, so we came up with a Not Porg Squash Roast.

MAKES: 4 TO 6 SERVINGS

2 small butternut squash,
1 tablespoon olive oil, divided
½ teaspoon kosher salt
2 small bunches of kale, divided
1 small shallot, minced
½ cup pomegranate arils
1 cup farro, cooked according to package directions, drained, and cooled

Dressing:

2 tablespoons good-quality olive oil
1 teaspoon pomegranate syrup
1 teaspoon rice wine vinegar
½ cup shaved parmesan (optional)

Special Supplies:

Melon baller

1. Preheat the oven to 375°F.

2. Cut each butternut squash in half from stem to bottom, lengthwise. Use a melon baller to scoop as much squash flesh from each half as possible without puncturing the outer wall.

3. Toss the squash pieces with about 2 teaspoons of the olive oil and ½ teaspoon of the salt. Use the remaining teaspoon of olive oil to rub the interior of each squash half, and sprinkle with a bit more salt.

4. Roast the squash in the oven for 7 to 10 minutes or until tender. The squash shells might need another 5 minutes; they are done when they're beginning to brown. Set aside the squash pieces and halves to cool.

5. Remove the stems from one kale bunch, leaving the leaves as whole as possible. Brush the kale lightly with about 1 tablespoon olive oil, and sprinkle with ½ teaspoon salt. Roast at 375°F for 3 to 5 minutes or until the kale is mostly dry and starting to crisp.

6. Remove the kale from the oven and allow it to cool completely on the cookie sheet. The kale pieces will continue to crisp as they cool. Gently remove the kale, store it in an airtight container, and set it aside.

7. Destem the remaining bunch of kale, cut it into ribbons, and wash and dry the ribbons.

8. Combine the kale, the roasted squash pieces, and all the dressing ingredients in a bowl with a pinch of salt. Massage the kale by hand, to mix thoroughly and tenderize the kale. Let the kale stand for 5 minutes.

9. To assemble: Mix the cooked faro and pomegranate arils into the kale/squash mixture, and serve in the roasted squash shells. Garnish with shaved parmesan, if using, and top with one or two kale chips.

PATIENCE LOST

In *Star Wars: The Clone Wars*, episode "Lightsaber Lost," Ahsoka Tano loses her lightsaber, and Jedi Master Tera Sinube helps her find it. This entire episode is about patience and how Ahsoka must slow down and quiet her mind in order to find her missing lightsaber.

Being a young Padawan, Ahsoka did not have much patience to begin with, but when a pickpocket stole her lightsaber, she panicked, and her patience disappeared. Ahsoka then tried to find her missing lightsaber on her own. She sought help from the Jedi Archives librarian Jocasta Nu, but when Jocasta came up empty-handed after searching the databanks, she recommended that Ahsoka speak to the elder Jedi Tera Sinube due to his expertise on the Coruscant crime world. Tera Sinube agreed to help Ahsoka, but they clashed when finding the thief: Ahsoka is very quick, sporadic, and made rash decisions, while Tera Sinube is slow, methodical, and thinks before she acts.

This episode is such an important lesson in patience. If Ahsoka did not listen to Master Sinube, she probably would not have found her lightsaber. Ahsoka was far too angry and worried to see or listen to the clues right in front of her. Master Sinube taught Ahsoka to slow down, quiet her mind, and have patience in order to find her lightsaber. Even though this story happened in a galaxy far, far away, the lessons learned in this episode can be applied to our real-life experiences. When we find ourselves in high-stress situations, we must *Stop*, *Think*, and *Act*. Here is how:

STOP: When our emotions are out of control, we cannot make rational decisions because we are acting on impulse (and our adrenaline is racing). So, stop and take a deep breath to calm your emotional response.

THINK: Now you can identify the problem. Why are you stressed, nervous, or angry in this moment? What's happening to you either physically or emotionally at this moment? What is the best way to solve this problem?

ACT: Finally, you can proceed with the best plan for the situation. And if you don't have a good plan, that's okay. Reach out to a trusted friend for their guidance and advice. Remember: It's okay to ask for help.

The next time you are in a high-stress situation remember to stop, think, and act.

HEARTS OF KYBER

In *Rogue One: A Star Wars Story*, Lyra Erso gives her daughter, Jyn, a kyber crystal necklace right before they are separated. When Lyra puts the necklace around Jyn's neck, she says, "Trust the Force." Jyn continues to wear this necklace as a token of good luck. At a pivotal moment in the film, we see Jyn clutch her kyber crystal pendant, as though she is using the Force to will the odds in her favor.

Now you can make your own kyber crystal necklace, to remind you to be patient and never lose hope. You might also want to make two necklaces and then give one to a friend or family member with a note that says, "Trust the Force."

WHAT YOU'LL NEED

- Glue stick
- Scissors
- Cutting mat or piece of cardboard
- Sharp craft knife
- Thin hemp cord
- Seed beads (any number or color)
- Hot glue gun
- Black cotton cord or leather cording

TIPS

- Make sure you're using a regular-size glue stick, not a mini stick.
- Never cut toward yourself yourself with the scissors or a knife.
- You can also use the kyber crystal to make a charm or keychain.

Let's Craft!

1. Using the scissors, cut the glue stick into thirds (each piece should be about 1½ inches long).

2. Hold the glue stick piece at the top and rest the bottom end on a cutting mat or thick piece of cardboard.

3. Use the craft knife to carefully slice thin pieces from the sides of the glue stick piece. Turn the glue stick piece as you cut until the entire piece resembles a crystal with faceted sides.

4. Flip the glue crystal to the other end and finish slicing the sides.

5. Cut a piece of the thin hemp cord 4 inches long, and tie a knot in one end.

6. String the seed beads in any pattern you like. Repeat for additional strings.

7. Hot-glue the bead strings at the top of the crystal, on the side.

8. Cut the black cotton cord or leather cording about 16 inches long. Hot-glue both ends to opposite sides at the top of the crystal.

9. Wrap the top of the crystal in the same cord you used for the bead. Glue down the end.

DARK SIDE

"FEAR IS THE PATH TO THE DARK SIDE.
FEAR LEADS TO ANGER.
ANGER LEADS TO HATE.
HATE LEADS TO SUFFERING."

Jedi Master Yoda, *The Phantom Menace*

CONFRONT YOUR FEARS

Throughout the *Star Wars* saga, we watch Anakin Skywalker fall to the dark side. The dark side is not a literal place or an organization, rather it's a lifestyle and belief system. Fear, anger, and hate are all things that can lead one to spiral into the dark side, and keeping a balance of light and dark is a constant practice that we all must be mindful of.

I've always connected with what Yoda says in the novelization of *Revenge of the Sith*, "Named your fear must be, before banish it you can." How can you overcome your fear if you don't know exactly what it is? In this next exercise, you will identify your fears and then confront them. Follow the steps below and face your fears . . . it is your destiny!

1. Take a blank piece of paper and write down your fear(s). If you are having trouble identifying your fears, talk it through with a trusted family member, friend, teacher, or counselor. Some questions to ask yourself that may help in identifying your fears might be:

   - What is something that brings you discomfort that you may avoid in your daily life?
   - What makes you feel powerless?
   - What makes you feel scared?
   - When are moments that you feel muscle tension or belly aches? Sometimes our fear presents itself as physical symptoms.

2. Once your fears are identified, confront them. This can be scary, and it takes great strength. But remember, to gain power over you fears you must have knowledge. Knowing and naming your fears is the first step in overcoming them. Ask yourself these questions:

   - Why do you have this fear? Is it realistic to have this fear? Is it true?
   - What is the worst-case scenario if your fears were to come true?
   - If the worst-case scenario happens, what would you do to move forward?
   - What actions would you take if your fear were to come true?

3. Now that your fears have been named, crumple up the piece of paper that your fears are written on into a small ball. This action symbolizes that you are making your fear smaller; you are diminishing it.

4. Now throw away (or recycle) your fear. Toss your fear in the trash, recycling bin, destroy it, banish it, etc. The physical act of getting rid of your fear can be very empowering.

Know that this exercise is not an instant cure for your fears. We must confront our fears by actually doing the thing that scares us. However, a repeated practice of facing your fears and an open dialogue about what you are afraid or worried about will make you stronger and diminish them over time.

A *STAR WARS* STRESS CHALLENGE

WHAT YOU'LL NEED

- A green balloon (Make sure it's deflated, not blown up.)
- 1 and ½ cups of sand, dry rice, beans, or lentils

In *Star Wars Rebels*, Ezra Bridger meets Jedi Master Yoda when he's suddenly pulled through a portal and into a world between worlds. Ezra seeks advice from Master Yoda on how to defeat Darth Vader and his Inquisitors. Yoda carefully warns Ezra not to become consumed by the dark side, just like the Jedi before him. Fear, anger, and hate could lead the Jedi, including Yoda, down a dark path. When Ezra appears surprised that Yoda fell victim to fear, Yoda responds, "A challenge lifelong it is, not to bend fear into anger."

This is very wise advice from Jedi Master Yoda, and it is wisdom that we can apply to our own lives as well. We all have fears—no one, not even Master Yoda, is immune to fear.

A great way to release the tension that builds within from stress and anger is with a fun stress ball: a bendable, squishable ball that we can squeeze in our hands. And for this exercise, we're going to make our own Yoda stress balls.

Let's Craft!

1. Fill the empty balloon with sand, rice, beans, or lentils, and tie the balloon once filled.

2. Once you have your stress ball, hold it in your hand. Close your eyes and think of your fear or whatever is causing you stress. Imagine yourself releasing that fear through your hands and into that stress ball. Really squeeze your stress out into the ball.

3. Keep squeezing your stress ball and while you are doing this, breath in through your nose for 4 seconds, hold your breath for 4 seconds and exhale out through your mouth for 4 seconds. Once you exhale, repeat aloud, "Try not. Do or do not. There is no try."

4. Repeat this as many times as needed until you feel yourself calm down.

DARK SIDE DECOR

The dark side is definitely a mood and a vibe. Although my personal mood and aesthetic is more inspired by the light side of the Force, life is a balance. Sometimes drawing inspiration from the dark side is fun when it comes to home decor, fashion, and food.

I've always loved the sleek look of the dark side: The iconic Death Star walls, with their vertical oval patterns and white backlighting behind them, are instantly recognizable. It's been a dream of mine to have a dark side accent wall like this in my home. It would also make an excellent photo op for your next *Star Wars* party! I turned to my friend Kelly to make my dark side decor dreams come true with this activity.

WHAT YOU'LL NEED

- ◆ Death Star Wall template
- Craft knife
- 1 black plastic corrugated board (20 by 30 inches)
- Masking tape
- Pencil
- Empty cereal box or similarly sized food packaging
- Ruler
- Hot glue gun
- Gray spray paint
- 1 white plastic corrugated board (20 by 30 inches)
- 1 string of battery-powered LED lights

TIPS

- Plastic corrugated boards are often available at craft stores.
- Be sure to place a cutting mat or cardboard underneath the plastic board as you cut.
- You can make just one or you can go on to make several, to turn a part of your home into a galactically cool photo background.

Let's Craft!

1. Begin by printing the Death Star Wall template from www.insighteditions.com/starwarseveryday

2. With the craft knife, cut out the oval shape from the template. Discard the oval shape.

3. Place the template on the black plastic corrugated board, lining up the left edge of the board with the left edge of the sheet. Tape the template in place.

4. Trace the oval shape on the black plastic corrugated board with a pencil. Lightly mark the top of the template sheet on the board with your pencil before removing the template.

5. Use the craft knife to carefully cut out the traced oval shape.

6. Place the template above the cut oval, again lining up the left edges. The bottom-left corner should line up with the mark you made in step 4. Trace and cut out the shape.

7. Repeat steps 3 through 6 until you reach the top. The top oval will extend past the top edge of the plastic corrugated board.

8. For the second column of ovals, begin on the bottom, with the template halfway off the bottom edge. The left edge of the template sheet should line up with the right edge of the ovals in the first column you cut.

9. Measure two pieces of cereal box or food packaging 11 inches long and 7½ inches wide. Use the scissors to cut out the two rectangles.

10. With the scissors, cut the box flaps and small rectangles from the remaining packaging.

11. Hot-glue the flaps and other small pieces on the unprinted side of the rectangles. Keep the edges of the small pieces parallel with the large rectangle edges.

12. Turn over the black plastic corrugated board so that the messier cut edges are on the back side. The ovals are now on the right side of the board.

13. Hot-glue the large rectangles to the left side of the black plastic corrugated board, again keeping the edges parallel.

14. It's time to paint! In a well-ventilated area, completely cover the black plastic corrugated board and cardboard rectangles with gray spray paint. Let everything dry.

15. Use the masking tape to stick the battery pack for the LED lights to the back side of the white plastic corrugated board.

16. Tape the string of LED lights to the front-left side of the white board. (The lights shouldn't show through the cut ovals later.)

17. Hot-glue the two plastic corrugated boards together so that the string of LED lights is sandwiched between them.

DRESS FOR THE DARK SIDE

George Lucas, the incredible creator of *Star Wars*, was heavily inspired by the Samurai culture of feudal Japan. He is also a huge fan of the famous Japanese film director Akira Kurosawa, and his films contain many Japanese influences, especially when it comes to Darth Vader.

Darth Vader's character draws heavily on influence from one of the most iconic warlords in Japanese history, Date Masamune—his distinguishable black armor became a muse for George Lucas as he created Darth Vader. However, the Samurai influences do not stop at Darth Vader. Several characters from *Star Wars*, such as the Jedi, draw inspiration from Samurai culture. When it comes to creating your own *Star Wars*—inspired costume or outfit, having a few staples in your closet will make it easy to dress the part.

A robe: Adding a black robe to your wardrobe makes it easy to dress for the dark side. I use Darth Maul's costume in *The Phantom Menace* as inspiration. I also recommend keeping a white, ivory, beige, or brown robe in your closet for the days when you want to dress like a Jedi.

A statement belt: Many *Star Wars* characters wear some sort of statement belt—think Darth Maul and Kylo Ren. For an instant dark side look, wear a thick black belt around your waist over top of your robe. Keep a thick brown belt in your closet for a Jedi look, too.

A cape: Capes are essential to the dark side. When Darth Vader walks down the hall, he exudes power; his cape is part of what makes him so formidable. Having some sort of black cape blazer, cape dress, or cape coat in your closet gives any outfit dark side vibes. Do not underestimate the power . . . of a cape!

Black boots: A staple for any wardrobe, especially a *Star Wars* wardrobe, is a pair of black boots. Most characters that associate with the dark side wear some sort of boot as footwear. Darth Vader, Darth Maul, and Kylo Ren all wear black knee-high boots for both practicality and protection. To make it a dark side look, wear a pair of black leggings or skinny jeans and boots. Keep a pair of knee-high brown boots in your closet, too, if you're feeling more light side that day.

WE HAVE COOKIES!

Fans of the dark side often jokingly say, "Come to the dark side . . . we have cookies." I'm not sure where this phrase originated, but as the foodie I am, I often wonder, *are the* cookies better on the dark side?

You know what they say: The way to a person's heart is through the stomach. Well, I wanted to test this theory, so I teamed up with my friend and expert baker Elena to create two tempting dark side cookie recipes. Be warned—these cookies are enticing, and you might find yourself pledging your allegiance to the dark side.

Kylo Crinkle Cookies

MAKES: ABOUT 3 DOZEN COOKIES

4 ounces bittersweet chocolate, chopped

1 cup unsweetened Dutch process cocoa

1¼ cups flour

2 teaspoons baking powder

¼ teaspoon kosher salt

1 teaspoon cinnamon, divided

½ teaspoon cayenne, divided

½ cup unsalted butter, softened

1½ cups packed dark brown sugar

2 large eggs

1 teaspoon vanilla extract

1 cup very hot water

1 cup granulated sugar

½ cup powdered sugar

½ cup black cocoa powder (see the following tip)

4 ounces red candy melt

1. In a microwave-safe bowl, in 30-second bursts, melt the bittersweet chocolate; set it aside.

2. In a medium bowl, sift together the Dutch process cocoa, flour, baking powder, and salt, along with ½ teaspoon cinnamon and ¼ teaspoon cayenne.

3. In the bowl of a stand mixer, or with a hand mixer, beat together the butter and brown sugar until light and fluffy.

4. Add the eggs one at time, mixing after each addition. Add the vanilla and melted chocolate, and mix to combine.

5. Add the flour mixture in two batches, alternating with the hot water. Divide the dough into four equal pieces. Wrap each one in parchment, and refrigerate for at least 2 hours.

6. When the dough has chilled, preheat the oven to 350°F, and prepare two baking sheets with baking mats or parchment.

7. Mix the remaining ½ teaspoon cinnamon and ¼ teaspoon cayenne into the granulated sugar in a medium bowl. Mix the powdered sugar and the black cocoa in another bowl, whisking to break up the clumps. Have both bowls standing by.

Continued on page 156

8. Working with one piece of dough at a time, create 1½-inch balls; then press them into an oval. Roll each oval in the sugar/spice mixture and then in the black cocoa mixture. Repeat until both cookie sheets are full.

9. Bake for 12 to 14 minutes until the cookie surfaces are cracked. Let the cookies cool on a wire rack.

10. Melt the red candy melt, and add it to a pastry or sealable bag. Snip a small opening in the tip of the bag and "repair" some of the cracks in each cookie. Allow the candy melt to set (about 15 minutes) before storing it in an airtight container. Cookies can be stored for up to 3 days.

Dark Side Chocolate Cookies

MAKES: ABOUT 3 DOZEN COOKIES

2 cups all-purpose flour

1 teaspoon baking soda

1 teaspoon salt

10 ounces extra-dark chocolate chips, divided

½ cup unsalted butter, cut into about 1-tablespoon chunks

4 teaspoons instant coffee

1 tablespoon vanilla

1 tablespoon hot water

1 cup dark brown sugar

2 eggs

1. Preheat the oven to 350°F, and prepare two baking sheets with either a silicone baking mat or parchment paper.

2. Combine all the dry ingredients, and set them aside.

3. In a microwave-safe bowl, add 1 cup of the extra-dark chocolate chips and the butter. Melt 30 seconds at a time until the butter is completely melted. Stir to completely melt the chocolate.

4. Dissolve the instant coffee into the vanilla and hot water, and stir it into the chocolate mixture.

5. Stir the sugar into the chocolate mixture, and combine thoroughly. Whisk in the eggs, one at a time.

6. Fold the chocolate mixture into the dry ingredients, and stir until everything is thoroughly combined. Add the remaining dark chocolate chips, and stir again.

7. Drop the cookies onto the prepared baking sheets with a 1½-inch scoop, 3 inches apart.

8. Bake for 12 to 14 minutes or until the tops feel set.

9. Allow the cookies to cool completely. It might take up to an hour for the chocolate chips to set.

SARLACC-O'-LANTERN

October is the perfect time to talk about all things pertaining to the dark side. The spooky season begins as we celebrate Halloween, so there's no better activity than a pumpkin craft for this haunted holiday. One of the crafts I look forward to every year at Halloween is pumpkin decorating. I always decorate a *Star Wars*–inspired pumpkin, and now you can, too!

The inspiration for this diorama is the infamous sarlacc pit from *Return of the Jedi*. After angering Jabba the Hutt, Luke Skywalker and Han Solo are sentenced to immediate death by being thrown into the Pit of Carkoon (the nesting place of the all-powerful sarlacc). Thankfully, our heroes narrowly escape the painful clutches of death, but several of Jabba's soldiers are not so lucky.

The following steps show you how to make your own Sarlacc-O'-Lantern pumpkin diorama. Happy carving!

WHAT YOU'LL NEED

- Small orange craft (foam) pumpkin
- Craft knife
- Hot glue gun
- Floral foam disc (approximately 5 by 1 inches)
- Floral foam ball (approximately 3 inches)
- Packing peanuts or scrap paper
- Foam modeling compound
- 7 toothpicks
- Craft foam sheet
- Scissors
- Red acrylic paint
- Tan acrylic paint
- Black acrylic paint
- Paintbrush
- Water
- Paint tray
- Gloss varnish
- Sand vase filler
- School glue
- Small spray bottle

Let's Craft!

1. Using the craft knife, cut out the top quarter of the pumpkin, around the stem. Discard or recycle the piece with the stem.

2. Hot-glue the foam disc to the bottom on the inside of the pumpkin. Hot-glue the foam ball to the center of the disc. The top of it should be situated just below the rim of the pumpkin.

3. Fill in the sides around the foam ball with packing peanuts or crumpled scrap paper. If you use packing peanuts, use crumpled paper for the top layer. The paper should sit just below the rim of the pumpkin, without covering it or the top of the foam ball.

4. Roll a chunk of foam modeling compound in a cylindrical shape. Press a toothpick into one end.

5. Shape the modeling foam into a tongue shape about 1½ inches long. Gently poke a toothpick in and out of the foam to create a tastebud texture. Set aside to dry.

6. Using scissors, cut a 2-inch pointed arch shape out of craft foam. Trace it on the foam, and cut a second pointed arch shape. These will form the sarlacc's head.

7. Paint the front and back of the arch with black acrylic paint. Let the paint dry.

Continued on page 158

TIPS

- Craft pumpkins aren't easy to cut! Take your time, to make sure the craft knife doesn't slip.

- Place the pumpkin on newspaper or cardboard when you pour the sand so that you can gather and reuse the overflow.

8. Paint the tongue with red acrylic paint, and let it dry.

9. Mix black paint and water on the paint tray (in about a 1:2 ratio of paint to water). Paint the tongue with the thinned black paint, to add depth to the texture.

10. When the tongue is dry, paint it with the glossy varnish.

11. Paint one side of each sarlacc head piece with the tan paint. Let the paint dry, and then paint the curved edges of both pieces tan.

12. Wrap the two head pieces around the tongue, hot gluing the straight bottom edges around the toothpick and tongue.

13. Press the toothpick end of the sarlacc into the foam ball.

14. Roll the modeling foam compound into six thin snake

shapes, about 3 inches long, to create the tentacles. Press a toothpick into the thick end of each. Curl the six tentacles into various curved shapes.

15. When the tentacles have dried, paint them with the tan acrylic paint.

16. Mix the black and tan paint on the paint tray, and add the darker color around the thick end of each tentacle. Let the paint dry.

17. Press the toothpick end of each tentacle into the foam ball around the sarlacc's head.

18. Roll very small and thin snakes of the modeling foam compound. Pull them apart into at least 20 small pieces, about ½ inches long, to make the sarlacc's pointy teeth. Set these aside to dry.

19. Slowly pour the craft sand around the sarlacc. The paper layer should catch most of the sand, but some will fall through. Arrange the sand into a mostly flat layer that covers the bottom of the sarlacc's head and tentacles.

20. Fill the small spray bottle a third full of school glue. Fill the remaining space with water, replace the top, and shake well.

21. Generously spray the sand layer with the glue mixture. Make sure the sand is completely covered with glue. Let the glue dry.

22. Check the sand again, and spray any loose particles with the glue mixture. Let everything dry.

23. When you're sure the sand is fixed in place, tip the pumpkin to remove any sand that fell through the cracks. Gather and save the sand for a future project.

24. Hot-glue the sarlacc's teeth all the way around the inside of the pumpkin, just below the rim.

25. Squeeze large drops of school glue down the sides of the pumpkin, and sprinkle sand over the glue. Let the glue dry.

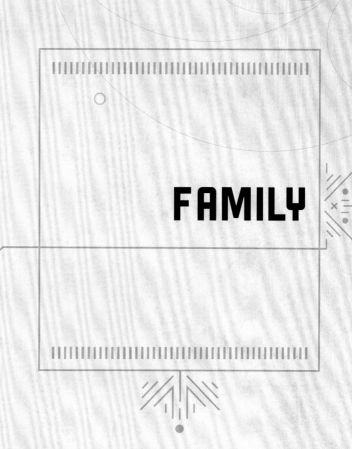

FAMILY

"BE WITH ME."

Rey, *The Rise of Skywalker*

A *MILLENNIUM FALCON* FAMILY

WHAT YOU'LL NEED

- ⬇ *Millennium Falcon* template, page 163
- Scissors
- Silver paint
- Paintbrush
- Crayons, markers, or pens, in various colors
- Silver marker
- White gel pen
- Black construction paper (8½ by 11 inches)
- White construction paper or printer paper
- Markers, in various colors
- School glue

TIP

Make the Aurebesh decoder (or make more than one) on page 133 before you begin this family project if you'd like to write anyone's names in Aurebesh. You can also download the template online at www.insighteditions.com/starwarseveryday.

Star Wars teaches us a lot about family. We learn that our family isn't just the one we're born with; it includes our found family, too—the friends we meet along the way who eventually become loved ones. This message takes center stage in *Star Wars* during Life Day, a Wookiee holiday that celebrates family, joy, and harmony. During this longstanding Wookiee tradition on November 17, everyone comes together to celebrate their dedication, courage, and love for one another.

This next activity highlights the people in your life, your chosen family. Instead of making a traditional family tree, you make a *Millennium Falcon* family. Han, Chewie, Luke, Leia, C-3PO, and R2-D2 became a family, or a crew, on the *Millennium Falcon*. Who would you take on board with you as your crew? Follow these instructions to create your own piece of *Star Wars* art!

Let's Craft!

1. Trace the *Millennium Falcon* template on page 163, and transfer it onto your white construction paper.

2. If you have any kids, family members, or those that you consider your "crew," have them create the *Falcon* with you. Use your imagination and creativity to color it in with any art supplies you like. You can even trace it on silver scrapbook paper and add details, or choose your own methods of decoration.

3. Add dots on the black paper with the white gel pen, to make a field of stars. Let the ink dry before the next step.

4. Give each member of your crew a piece of white paper. Ask everyone to use a silver marker and/or white gel pen to write their name in Aurebesh and then decorate it.

5. If you'd like, you can also cut out pictures of your crew members, and glue them to the *Falcon*.

6. Glue the *Millennium Falcon* to the black paper; then glue the names of the crew on the ship.

A SYMBOL OF FAMILY NECKLACE

WHAT YOU'LL NEED

- Gold polymer clay
- Clay roller
- Two clay circle cutters, one ½ inch and one 1½ inch in diameter
- Clay shaping tools
- Toothpick
- Gold acrylic paint
- Paintbrush
- Black acrylic paint
- Water
- Paint tray
- Paper towel
- 2 open jump rings
- Needle-nose or jewelry pliers
- 2 necklace chains or pieces of string, 18 inches long

TIPS

- Polymer clay can damage furniture. Prepare your work surface with plastic or aluminum foil.
- Polymer clays are kid safe and nontoxic, but check the product packaging before you use them.
- Keep one medallion for yourself and give the other to a friend or loved one.

In *The Last Jedi*, we meet Paige Tico, a Resistance pilot who sacrifices her life to help take out an Imperial Dreadnought. Right before she loses her life in an explosion, Paige clutches a small medallion of Haysian smelt that she wears around her neck. Later in the movie, we meet Rose Tico, a Resistance mechanic and Paige's sister, as she mourns the loss of her sister while crying and clutching the other half of the same medallion. This medallion is a beautiful symbol of family: When the two sides are put together, they represent the emblem of the Otomok system, the sisters' home.

Throughout *The Last Jedi*, we watch Rose and Finn go on an epic adventure to save the Resistance. Along the way, they become each other's found family. At the end of the film, Rose saves Finn from sacrificing his own life and teaches us an important lesson about love: "That's how we're going to win. Not fighting what we hate, saving what we love." This is a beautiful reminder to always keep our focus on love, not hate. And as we have learned from *Star Wars*, hate is a path to the dark side.

Now you can make your own Otomok system emblem medallion, just like the one shared by the Tico sisters!

Let's Craft!

1. Break off a chunk of gold polymer clay and gently knead it to warm it up.

2. With the clay roller, roll out the clay no more than ½ centimeter thick. Cut out a circle with the 1½-inch clay circle cutter.

3. Press the ½-inch circle cutter at the top and bottom of the 1½-inch clay circle, without cutting all the way through.

4. Use a sharp-edged clay tool to cut a curved line from the left side of the top circle to the right side of the bottom circle. The design should resemble two connected leaf shapes.

5. Gently pull apart the two leaf shapes.

6. Use a toothpick to press a hole through the pointed ends of the pendants.

7. Use a sharp-edged clay tool to carve a round line just above the small circle in the pendant.

8. Carve a triangular shape in the top half of the pendant. Carve crisscrossing lines inside.

9. Roll five tiny balls of gold polymer clay, about the size of a pinhead. Press two balls inside the triangle shape where lines cross. Press three balls inside the small circle.

10. Place the pendants on a foil-lined baking sheet. Bake according to the polymer clay instructions. Remove the pendants from the oven and let them cool.

11. Paint the pendants with gold acrylic paint. Let the paint dry completely.

12. Mix the black paint and water in a 1:2 ratio on a paint tray.

13. Paint the pendants with the watery paint mix. Soak up any excess paint by dabbing with a paper towel. Let the paint dry.

14. Open a jump ring with the pliers, and pass it through the hole on the pendant. Close the ring with the pliers. Repeat for the second pendant.

15. Slide the pendant onto a necklace chain or string. Repeat for the second pendant.

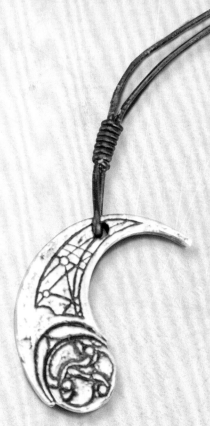

SKYWALKER FAMILY RECIPES

Some of my favorite foods come from family recipes that have been passed down by generations. Others are recipes that only a loved one can make because of that special touch. I get a feeling of comfort and nostalgia when I eat my Grandma Juliet's meatballs, my dad's turkey stuffing, or my mom's twice baked potatoes. Nothing beats the time we spend with family while sitting around a dining table and sharing a meal. I would imagine that our *Star Wars* heroes have their favorite family recipes, too!

Aunt Beru's Harvest Bake

In *A New Hope*, we see Aunt Beru, Uncle Owen, and Luke Skywalker sit down for a meal together. We don't exactly see what they're eating, but I like to imagine that it's some sort of specialty casserole made by Aunt Beru. The following is Elena's recipe inspired by the dish Aunt Beru made in the film. This is the perfect meal to make as families come together during the holidays. Oh, and if the kids complain about eating their vegetables, just tell them that this was Luke Skywalker's favorite meal!

MAKES: 6 SERVINGS

Cauliflower Purée:

2 garlic cloves, peeled

2 heads romanesco cauliflower, broken up into small florets

1 cup vegetable broth

¾ cup (about 2 ounces) crumbled cotija cheese

Filling:

2 teaspoons kosher salt, divided

1 yellow onion, diced

4 garlic cloves, diced

2 tablespoons olive oil

12 ounces mushrooms, sliced

1 teaspoon sumac

1½ pounds ground beef (or cashews—see the following tip)

1 cup frozen green peas

Plant-Based Option (Instead of Ground Beef):

1 cup raw cashews

1 cup boiling water

Continued on page 168

1. In a large pot fitted with a steamer basket, and filled with water to just under the basket, bring to a boil. Place the garlic and cauliflower florets in the steamer basket, and steam for about 20 minutes or until very tender. Drain the garlic and cauliflower, and let them cool for 5 minutes.

2. Combine the garlic and cauliflower in a food processor, pulsing a few times to chop.

3. Add the vegetable broth, and pulse until the mixture is mostly smooth.

4. Add the crumbled cheese, and pulse briefly to combine. Set aside the puree while you prepare the filling.

5. Have a 9-by-13-inch casserole dish standing by. Preheat the oven to 375°F.

6. For the filling, in a large sauté pan, combine half of the salt with the onions and garlic; sauté this until translucent. Add the mushrooms and the sumac, stir to combine, and continue to sauté until the mushrooms are tender, about 5 to 7 minutes. Remove the mushroom mixture to the casserole dish.

7. Brown the ground beef with the remaining teaspoon of salt and black pepper to taste. Cook until all the beef is cooked through, about 5 minutes.

8. Add the beef to the casserole dish and stir to combine with the mushroom mixture.

9. Add in the peas and stir again. Spread the cauliflower purée over the filling mixture, and bake for 30 to 40 minutes or until heated through and browning on top.

FOR A PLANT-BASED OPTION:

1. Put the cashews in a heat-proof bowl, cover them with water, and let them soak for 10 minutes.

2. Drain the cashews, reserving 2 tablespoons of the soaking water.

3. When the mushroom mixture is ready, stir the cashews and the soaking liquid in with the peas; then proceed with steps 6 through 9.

Shmi Skywalker's Oats

In *The Phantom Menace*, a young Anakin Skywalker meets Qui-Gon Jinn, Padmé Amidala, Jar-Jar Binks, and R2-D2 while working with the junk dealer Watto. With an impending sandstorm approaching, Anakin welcomes his new friends to the home that he shares with his mother, Shmi Skywalker. While they wait out the storm, Shmi serves everyone a meal that they eat together.

We don't exactly know what Shmi made, but it looks like some sort of slow-cooked oats. We can also see a bowl of fruit on the table, and Jar-Jar can't resist helping himself to what looks like apples. Shmi made a warm and comforting food that our heroes needed to wait out the storm. The next time you have guests over for breakfast, serve them this simple but delicious recipe. You can prepare the recipe the night before and cook it in a slow cooker overnight, and it will be ready to eat when you wake up! It's like comfort in a bowl and a hug from Anakin's mom.

MAKES: 4 TO 6 SERVINGS

2 cups oat milk, plus more for serving

2 cups water

2 cups dried oats

1 whole cinnamon stick

2 apples, peeled, cored, and diced, plus more for garnish

Walnuts or pecans (optional)

Special Supplies:

Slow cooker

1. Combine the oat milk and water. Add the oats and diced apples, and stir again to combine. Place the cinnamon stick on top.

2. Set the slow cooker to low for 8 hours.

3. To serve: Add the extra chopped apples (with the peel left on), nuts (if using), and more oat milk available for topping.

TIP

If you have a large-capacity slow cooker (more than 2 quarts), set it to cook on low for 1½ hours. You can leave it on warm for up to 8 hours.

STAR WARS LUNCH BOX NOTES

One of my favorite childhood memories was having my mom leave surprise notes in my school lunch box. Her notes were short and encouraging, and these motivational messages always made my day.

The *Star Wars* universe is a treasure trove for positive messages of wisdom. Personally, I look to the quotes at the beginning of each episode of *Star Wars: The Clone Wars* when I'm searching for thought-provoking advice. I love the lessons they inspire.

For this next activity, I list some of my favorite quotes from the beginning of each season of *Star Wars: The Clone Wars*. Feel free to use the following quotes and leave surprise lunch box notes for the kids (or kids at heart!) in your life. Then at night around the dinner table or before bed, discuss what the quote means and how it relates to everyday life.

"Great leaders inspire greatness in others."

Star Wars: The Clone Wars, "Ambush"

"Our actions define our legacy."

Star Wars: The Clone Wars, "Carnage of Krell"

"Never give up hope, no matter how dark things seem."

Star Wars: The Clone Wars, "The Wrong Jedi"

"If there is no path before you, create your own."

Star Wars: The Clone Wars, "Gone with a Trace"

"BE WITH ME" BREATHING EXERCISE

The last two months of the year can be tough for anyone who's unable to spend the holidays with the ones they care about most. Whether a loved one is away or has passed on, the holidays can be an extremely difficult time of year for some people. But in *Star Wars*, we learn that no one is ever really gone. We' are all connected through the Force, and even though we might not be able to see them or feel them, we are still connected by their energy and their wisdom.

At the beginning of *The Rise of Skywalker*, we find Rey practicing a Jedi training exercise. She's floating while meditating and reciting "Be with me," reaching out to other Jedi in the hopes of hearing their voices. She doesn't sense that the Jedi are with her, so she loses her patience and gives up. But, when Rey is fighting Emperor Palpatine, she tries connecting with the other Jedi again, and it works! She hears the voices of Yoda, Obi-Wan Kenobi, Anakin Skywalker, Qui-Gon Jinn, and Ahsoka Tano, among others. These characters tell Rey to rise and get back up. They remind her that she is not alone, that the Jedi live inside her, and that the Force is with her.

That's a lot to digest, but here's the lesson: Even though this story takes place in a galaxy far, far away, we are all connected through the Force. We might not be able to move things with a Force push, float in the air, or perform a Jedi mind trick, but I believe we are all connected. The wisdom of our loved ones, both past and present, will always be with us in our hearts and in our minds.

1. Sit in a quiet and calm space, such as your meditation space (page 135). Sit with your legs crossed, or in whatever position is comfortable for you, and close your eyes.

2. Place your palms up, and slightly reach out as though you are connecting with the Force and the energy around you.

3. Take in a deep breath, exhale, and say aloud, "Be with me."

4. Visualize your loved one—someone who is not with you presently or someone who has passed on. See your loved one and hear that person in your mind. Think of a positive memory, something that person taught you.

What advice would they give you right now? How would they want you to carry on?

5. Repeat steps 1 through 4 when needed, and continue to think of the same loved one or multiple loved ones that you want to connect with until you feel their presence in your heart and your mind.

> **TIP**
>
> This exercise can be very emotional, and I recommend practicing this with someone or talking to a loved one or family member afterwards for support.

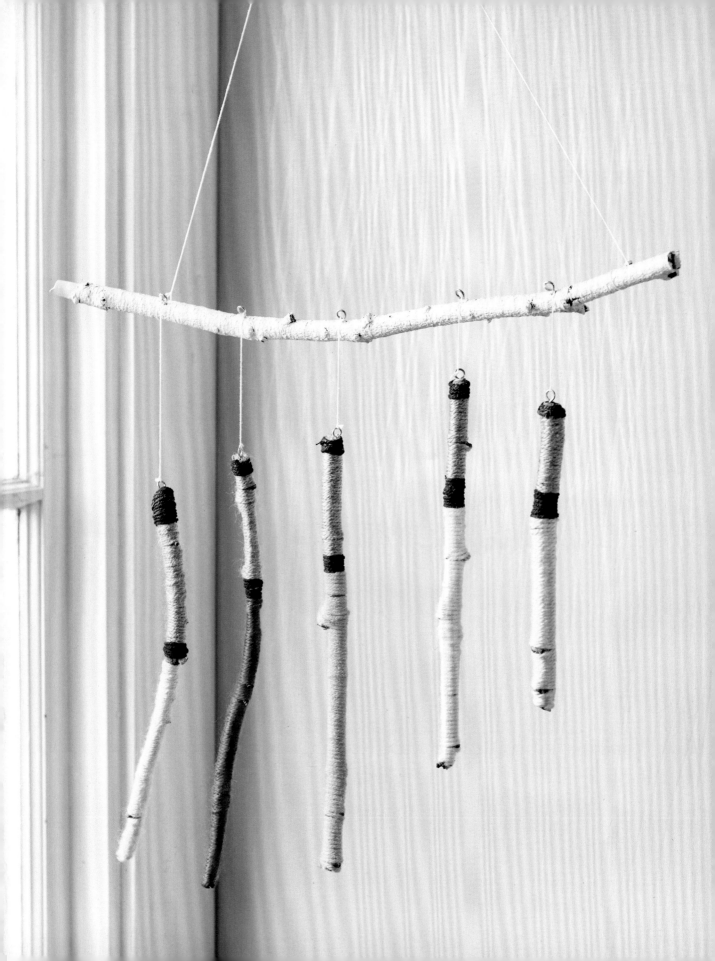

LIGHTSABER HANGING DISPLAY

When we first meet Rey in *The Force Awakens*, we discover that she is a scavenger. Rey lives in an old, abandoned AT-AT walker, and when we get a glance at her makeshift home, we see that she once made a rebel pilot doll out of scraps (so cool!). This is a great reminder for younglings and adults alike that one person's trash can be another person's treasure. As we enter the season of gift giving, homemade gifts are often most cherished because of the amount of thought and care that goes into creating them.

This is the perfect craft for young Padawans to make (with help from an adult, of course). Follow the instructions to make this hanging display for a child's room or to give as a gift!

Let's Craft!

1. Go outside and find six dry sticks about the same thickness as your finger. One should be about 14 inches long; the others should decrease in length, starting at 11 inches. Snap off any small twigs from the sticks you've gathered.

2. Paint the long 14-inch stick with white acrylic paint, and let it dry.

3. Twist two screw eyes on either end of the white stick; the display will hang from here.

4. Twist five screw eyes, evenly spaced, on the opposite side.

5. Twist a screw eye into the thicker "hilt" end of the five sticks you gathered.

6. Add a small amount of glue to the thicker end of the stick. Wrap the silver yarn around the base of the stick until you cover about 3 inches of space; then cut and glue down the end.

7. Wrap a small amount of black yarn around the top and bottom of the silver section.

8. Choose a color for the lightsaber blade. Add a small amount of glue to the stick, and wrap the colored yarn until the stick is completely covered. Cut and glue down the end.

9. Repeat steps 6 through 8 for every stick until you have five yarn-wrapped lightsabers.

10. Tie a piece of string about 6 inches long to the hook in the largest lightsaber. Tie it to the first hook on the white stick.

11. Continue tying the lightsabers to the white stick, largest to smallest, with the string length also decreasing as you go.

12. Tie a piece of string about 12 inches long to the two hooks on top of the white stick. Your mobile is now ready to hang.

WHAT YOU'LL NEED

- 1 thick stick, about 14 inches long
- White acrylic paint
- Paintbrush
- 12 small screw eyes
- School glue
- 5 thick sticks, decreasing in length
- Silver yarn
- Black yarn
- Light blue yarn
- Light green yarn
- Yellow yarn
- Purple yarn
- Scissors
- Thin string

TIPS

- Add a drop of glue to the base of each screw eye, to reinforce the grip.
- Hold the string of yarn in one hand, and rotate the stick in the other to evenly wrap it.
- Do not hang this mobile above a baby's crib.

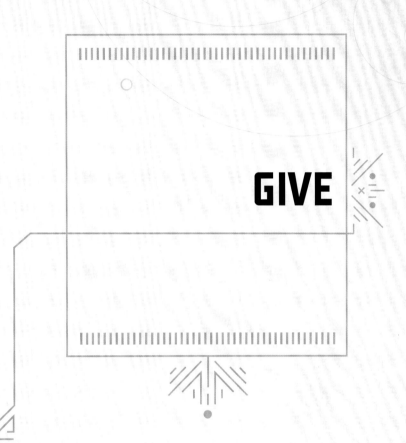

GIVE

"WE HAD EACH OTHER.
THAT'S HOW WE WON."

Lando Calrissian, *The Rise of Skywalker*

BOBA'S BOUNTY

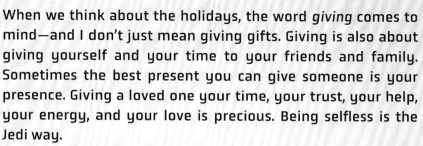

When we think about the holidays, the word *giving* comes to mind—and I don't just mean giving gifts. Giving is also about giving yourself and your time to your friends and family. Sometimes the best present you can give someone is your presence. Giving a loved one your time, your trust, your help, your energy, and your love is precious. Being selfless is the Jedi way.

The first activity for this month is all about giving. It provides a fun way to give gifts to your family, but the real gift is the lessons you learn and the joy and laughter you share together. This new holiday tradition, which I'm calling Boba's Bounty, helps you do just that. As one of the most famous bounty hunters in *Star Wars*, Boba Fett is hired to go on missions; when he completes a mission, he receives a fee, or a *bounty*.

For this activity, an adult or guardian can create the Boba Fett helmet craft by following the instructions on page 178. After the helmet is made, it should mysteriously appear each morning, for seven straight days, with a mission for everyone in the house to complete.

You can write each mission on an index card. On one side of the card, write a large letter, such as the letter *R*. On the other side of the card, write a task that everyone has to do that day. At the end of the day, each person in the family must come back to Boba and share how they completed the task. If everyone completes the task, Boba returns the next morning with a bounty and a new task.

WHAT YOU'LL NEED

- ⬇ Boba Fett Helmet template
- Scissors
- Sewing pins
- Olive green felt
- Sewing needle
- Olive green thread
- Batting
- Red adhesive-backed felt
- Black adhesive-backed felt
- Pencil
- School glue

TIP

Get creative with the bounty—it can be a gift, a sweet treat, or something practical for the whole family. Have fun with it!

CARD TEMPLATES:

Day 1: On the front of the card, write the letter *R*. On the back of the card, write the mission: *Remember to say "thank you" to everyone who helps you today.*

Day 2: On the front of the card, write the letter *E*. On the back of the card, write the mission: *Explain to someone how much you appreciate them and why.*

Day 3: On the front of the card, write the letter *S*. On the back of the card, write the mission: *Show gratitude today. Find there things in your life that you're grateful for.*

Day 4: On the front of the card, write the letter *P*. On the back of the card, write the mission: *Be "present" for someone today. Ask them how they are doing, and really listen to their answers.*

Day 5: On the front of the card, write the letter *E*. On the back of the card, write the mission: *Encourage someone today. Ask someone to tell you a goal or dream for the new year, and offer encouragement to make it happen.*

Day 6: On the front of the card, write the letter *C*. On the back of the card, write the mission: *Call someone to say happy holidays and let them know you're thinking of them.*

Day 7: On the front of the card, write the letter *T*. On the back of the card, write the mission: *Treat others as you would want to be treated. Do something for someone today that you would want done for you.*

Continued on page 178

Let's Craft!

1. Download and print the helmet template from www.insighteditions.com/ starwarseveryday. Cut out the pieces with scissors.

2. Use the sewing pins to pin the large helmet template to the green felt. Cut out the shape from the felt. Repeat to make a second piece.

3. Pin the two helmet shapes together.

4. Thread a needle with the olive-green thread, and sew around the bottom-left corner, all the way around to the bottom-right corner. (You won't be flipping the shape inside out, so make your stitches nice and even.)

5. Stuff the helmet with batting, taking care not to rip any of your stitches.

6. Sew the bottom edge of the helmet closed with the olive-green thread.

7. Trace the wide visor shape on the paper backing of the red adhesive felt. Cut it out.

8. Trace the thin *T*-visor shape on the paper backing of the black adhesive felt. Cut it out.

9. Remove the backing on the *T* shape, and stick it to the red felt visor, lining up the two shapes with the bottom edge.

10. Remove the backing on the red visor shape, and stick it to the

helmet, lining it up with the center of the bottom edge.

11. Cut four small strips of red felt, about ½ inch long. Stick them, evenly spaced, just above the visor next to the right edge.

12. Glue down any edges or corners of felt that aren't completely secure. Let the glue dry.

TIP

If necessary, you can use glue instead of a needle and thread on the green felt pieces. However, glue might not hold as strongly as thread.

JAWA JINGLE HOLIDAY PARTIES

Nothing brings people together quite like *Star Wars*. Whether you're a casual enthusiast or a passionate fan, everyone has a memory or a story about their connection to this iconic franchise. That's why, when it comes to throwing a holiday party, there's no better theme than *a Star Wars* party! The following are ideas for your next *Star Wars* holiday party. Enjoy!

Holiday Cookie Party

Growing up, my mom threw holiday cookie exchange parties in which everyone brought three dozen of their favorite cookie and an empty take home container. A holiday cookie party is the perfect opportunity to bake and give the Cookies for Wookiees from this chapter, page 181, or the Dark Side Chocolate Cookies, page 156. Serve some Sithmas Sips (page 181) during the cookie exchange, and your holiday party will be off to a great start!

Jawa Gift Trade

In *Star Wars*, Jawas are known for their trading. They sell and trade their refurbished goods, but they're also known for trying to pawn something off as more valuable than it really is. A Jawa Gift Trade, similar to a "white elephant" gift exchange, is the perfect way to exchange gifts at your *Star Wars* holiday party. Here's how to host a Jawa Gift Trade:

1. Ask all your guests to bring a wrapped, anonymous gift. The gift should be something they already own that they no longer use or something they have extras of.

2. Have everyone write a clue about their gift on a card, and tape that card to the outside of the gift. Make sure everyone writes down a clue, not the actual name of the gift. Place the gifts in a pile in the middle of the room or on a table so everyone can see all the presents.

3. Count the number of guests you have and write out the numbers on little pieces of paper. Place the numbers in a bag. Have each person draw a number. The person who draws #1 gets the first pick. They must pick a gift and read the clue out loud; however, they must not open the gift. The gifts will be opened together at the very end of the game. Then the person who drew #2 has the option to trade for person #1's gift; alternatively, they can pick a new gift from the pile. This continues until each person has picked a present.

4. As more presents are picked, your guests will have the option to trade with anyone who has already picked a present, or they can choose from the gifts that are left in the pile.

5. After the last person picks their gift, the person who drew #1 has the final option to trade, or they can keep the gift they have. Finally, starting with #1, each person reads their clue out loud once more and opens the gift they chose. Happy trading!

COOKIES FOR WOOKIEES (& MILK)

I was raised with an Italian grandmother who was always in the kitchen baking something delicious. Every year during the holidays, she gave us a big box filled with multiple tins of cookies. Now that my Grandma Juliet has passed, the rest of the family has carried on her tradition. We have a cookie baking day every December, and we bake hundreds of cookies. As a massive *Star Wars* fan, I naturally incorporate Cookies for Wookiees (& Milk) into the mix. I'm sure Santa appreciates a *Star Wars*–inspired snack break when he stops by our house! Let's stir, whip, stir, whip, whip, whip, stir, and bake some Cookies for Wookiees!

Sithmas Sip

You simply can't have Cookies for Wookiees without milk. Milk and cookies are a package duo, and blue milk and green milk have become iconic *Star Wars* drinks. However, just like when we go to a coffee shop, we have our choice of multiple different kinds of milks. We can choose from cow's milk, soy milk, coconut milk, almond milk, oat milk, and beyond. I imagine that choice would be the same in a galaxy far, far away, so we created a red milk recipe, called Sithmas Sip, that's perfect for the holidays. This drink pairs perfectly with the cookies from this book and will keep Santa coming back year after year.

MAKES: 4 TO 6 DRINKS

1 teaspoon whole cloves

2 cinnamon sticks

1 cup sugar

2 cups pure, unsweetened cranberry juice

1 cup unsweetened vanilla coconut milk (in a carton, not a can)

1. Combine all the ingredients in a medium saucepan and bring to a simmer. Stir until the sugar is dissolved.

2. Remove from heat and let steep with the spices until cool.

3. Strain into a container, seal, and refrigerate until serving. To serve, reheat by the mug-full in the microwave, or heat it in a saucepan.

Gingerbread Character Cookies

MAKES: ABOUT 2 DOZEN COOKIES

Dough:

6 cups sifted all-purpose flour

1 teaspoon baking soda

½ teaspoon baking powder

1 cup unsalted butter, softened

1 cup packed dark brown sugar

1 tablespoon ground ginger

1 teaspoon ground cardamom

4 teaspoons cinnamon

1 teaspoon fine freshly ground black pepper

1 teaspoon allspice

½ teaspoon clove

1½ teaspoons kosher salt

2 large eggs

1 cup molasses

Icing:

3 tablespoons meringue powder

4 cups powdered sugar, sifted

6 tablespoons water

Food coloring

Special Supplies:

Food coloring

Pastry bags and tips

Gingerbread man and gingerbread woman cookie cutters, in various sizes

Teddy bear cookie cutter, small

Egg cookie cutter

1. In a large bowl, combine the sifted flour, baking soda, and baking powder. Set this bowl aside.

2. In the bowl of an electric mixer fitted with the paddle attachment, cream the butter and sugar until light and fluffy. Mix in spices and salt from the dough ingredients.

3. Add the eggs and molasses, and mix well. With the machine on low speed, gradually add the flour mixture, and beat until combined.

4. Divide the dough into thirds, and wrap each piece of dough in parchment. Chill for at least 1 hour.

5. Preheat the oven to 350°F. Line the baking sheets with silicone baking mats or parchment paper, and set them aside.

6. On a lightly floured work surface, roll out dough to ¼ inch thick. Cut out various character shapes. Use the small gingerbread woman cutter to create Yoda by trimming the head down to a low mound and pinching the arms so they become his pointy ears. To make Chewbacca (or other Wookiees), use a large gingerbread man cookie cutter. To create the Ahsoka cookie, pinch the top of a gingerbread boy to create her "lekku." To create the porg cookies, use different sizes of egg cookie cutters utilizing a paring knife to make the side slits, creating the wings.

7. Transfer the cookies to the prepared baking sheets, and chill in the refrigerator for at least 15 minutes before baking. (This allows the dough to keep its shape and prevents spreading.) Bake the cookies in the oven for 9 to 12 minutes or until slightly browned and firm to the touch. Remove the cookies from the oven and allow them to cool completely before decorating.

8. To make the icing: Beat all the ingredients in a stand mixer at low speed for 7 to 10 minutes, or with a hand mixer at high speed for 10 to 12 minutes. Divide the icing into small bowls, and use food coloring to create your desired colors. Transfer the icing to pastry bags or sealable bags, and decorate as desired. Allow the cookies to dry completely before serving, packaging, or storing (at least 3 hours).

Chewie Peanut Butter Sandwich Cookies

MAKES: ABOUT 24 COOKIES

Dough:

10 tablespoons butter, softened
½ cup chunky peanut butter
½ cup brown sugar, firmly packed
1 egg
2 cups all-purpose flour

Filling:

1 cup smooth peanut butter
3 tablespoons powdered sugar
1 tablespoon black cocoa powder

Special Equipment:

Round cookie cutter, about 2½ inches in diameter
Parchment
Pastry bag
White jimmies (or long, tubed-shape sprinkles)

TIPS

- Cookies can be baked ahead, stored in an airtight container, and frozen for up to 1 month. Defrost them, fill them, and decorate them when you're ready to serve.

- If you are allergic to peanuts, use sunflower seed butter instead.

1. In the bowl of a stand mixer, combine the butter, chunky peanut butter, and sugar, and beat until combined. Add the egg, and beat again. Add the flour, and mix until all the flour is incorporated and a dough starts to form.

2. Split the dough in half, and work with one half at a time. Place each half between 2 pieces of parchment, and roll it out to ¼ inch thick. Use the cookie cutter to cut out as many rounds as possible. Remove the scraps, leaving the rounds on the parchment, and add them back to the other dough.

3. Roll the second half, plus scraps, between the parchment, and cut out more rounds. Reroll the scraps as needed.

4. Texture the surface of each round with a fork, to add fur. Place the rounds, on their parchment, on a cookie sheet; refrigerate the rounds for 10 minutes.

5. Preheat the oven to 350°F while the rounds are chilling.

6. Bake the cookies for 12 to 14 minutes until the edges are browning and the centers feel firm. Allow to cool completely.

7. To prepare the filling, combine all the ingredients in a small bowl, and mix thoroughly with a fork.

8. To assemble: Spread a thin layer of filling on half of the cookies, and top with a second cookie. Put the remaining filling in a pastry bag, snip off the end, and pipe a diagonal line across each sandwich. Add jimmies along the line. Allow to set for 10 minutes before storing in an airtight container for 3 days.

HOLIDAY "STAR" WARS ORNAMENT

When it comes to decorating for the holidays, I love to decorate with stars. I have star ornaments and a star tree topper on my tree, I have stars in my outdoor holiday decorations—I basically have stars everywhere! I try to combine my love of stars with my love of *Star Wars* in my holiday decor—not just because of the name *Star Wars*, but also because the Death Star has become one of the most iconic stars in the galaxy. From decor, to gifts, to parties, I love incorporating *Star Wars* into my holiday plans.

This next craft is the perfect activity to do whether you're part of a group or by yourself. You also can make a bunch of these and give them out as gifts. This homemade Death "Star" makes a beautiful *Star Wars* ornament or, depending on the size of your tree, the perfect tree topper. This craft is great for kids, too, with adult supervision.

Let's Craft!

1. Measure a piece of the red and gold glitter paper 4 inches long and ½ inch wide. Cut it out with the scissors.

2. Fold the strip you just made in half, and glue the ends together. Gently bend the paper into a flower petal shape.

3. Repeat steps 1 and 2 until you have eight petal-shape strips.

4. Hot-glue all eight petal shapes together to form a flower shape, starting with two petals glued end to end. Glue the next two petals perpendicular to the first two, and then fill in the remaining petals evenly.

5. Cut the two gold paper straws in half. Glue them between the petals to make an X shape.

6. Cut the gold chenille stem in half. Hot-glue the stems on opposite sides between the gold straws.

7. Cut a piece of string about 4 inches long. Tie the ends together to make a loop; glue it at the knot between two of the petals.

8. Cut one 1½-inch circle and one ⅝-inch circle from the metallic silver cardstock.

9. Use the school glue to attach the smaller circle to the top left of the larger circle. This will be the "dish" of the Death Star.

10. With the white gel pen, draw small dots for the Death Star's lights on the larger silver circle. Let the ink dry.

11. Hot-glue the Death Star to the center of the ornament, with the string on the same top side as the dish.

12. Repeat steps 8 through 11 to add a Death Star to the other side of the ornament.

CRAFTY COASTERS

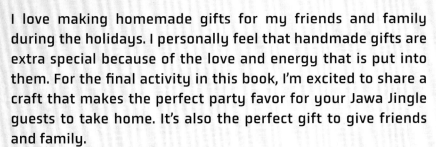

I love making homemade gifts for my friends and family during the holidays. I personally feel that handmade gifts are extra special because of the love and energy that is put into them. For the final activity in this book, I'm excited to share a craft that makes the perfect party favor for your Jawa Jingle guests to take home. It's also the perfect gift to give friends and family.

This craft is fairly inexpensive, and you can make several coasters from one picture book. I love my handmade coasters, and I use them every time we eat dinner at home—and I think of my family every time I use them. I recommend that you make sets of two or four coasters, to give as presents.

Let's Craft!

1. Measure a 3½-by-3½-inch square on the cardboard, and cut it out with scissors. This will be the template for your coaster.

2. Find a page in the book you've chosen with a picture you think the recipient (or you) will appreciate, such as a favorite scene or character. Cut the page from the book using scissors.

3. Place the cardboard template over the picture, and trace it. Cut out the traced square.

4. Flip the picture over to the back side. Divide the square into fours by measuring and drawing lines halfway (1¾ inches) up from the bottom and left sides.

5. Cut out the four squares.

6. Use the paintbrush to add a very thin layer of decoupage glue on the back side of the bottom-left square. Stick the square to the tile.

7. Repeat with the other square pieces, leaving a small but even gap between each image.

8. Brush the decoupage glue in a thin layer across the top of the tile. Remove any folds or bubbles in the paper as you press down with the brush. (Don't press too hard, or the paper will tear!)

9. Repeat steps 2 through 8 with the other three pages and ceramic tiles. Let the glue dry.

10. Choose a color for the vinyl sheet that matches the picture you selected. Add small designs to the coaster by cutting and sticking the vinyl; for example, you could create thin stripes or make dots using the paper hole punch.

11. Add another thin layer of decoupage glue on top of the coaster, and let that dry completely.

12. Choose a color of felt that matches the picture. Trace the cardboard template on the felt, and cut it out.

13. Flip the coaster to the back side. Glue the felt square to the back side, and let it dry completely.

WHAT YOU'LL NEED

- Scrap cardboard or cardstock
- Pencil
- Ruler
- Scissors
- *Star Wars* picture book
- Paintbrush
- Decoupage glue
- Four white ceramic tiles (4 by 4 inches)
- Adhesive vinyl sheet (any color)
- Paper hole punch
- Felt (any color)

TIPS

- You can find ceramic tiles at any home improvement store.
- If you don't have old picture books, then magazines or comic books work well, too.
- Find books and pictures that feature the recipient's favorite *Star Wars* moments and characters (or yours!).

A NOTE FROM ASHLEY

Thank you so much for joining me in bringing *Star Wars* into your homes and your everyday lives all year long. Throughout this journey, you have learned, trained, played, created, eaten, drunk, laughed, cried, loved, hoped, and become one with the Force. I hope you'll continue to embrace *Star Wars* and include it in your everyday life. Come back to this book on a regular basis to repeat these exercises, activities, crafts, and recipes. Make sure to save room for your own *Star Wars* traditions, too! The stories and themes from *Star Wars* can be lifechanging if you let them. Hold these lessons in your heart and soul, and wear them like armor as you go out and face each day.

Before Yoda became one with the Force in *Return of the Jedi*, he said to Luke Skywalker, "Always pass on what you have learned." I firmly believe that we should carry this reminder with us. After reading this book, I hope that you will take all these themes with you: hope, love, discipline, friendship, celebration, adventure, discovery, power, patience, the dark side, family, and giving. Learn them well, and pass these lessons on to the next generation of *Star Wars* fans. Remember, the Force will be with you . . . always!

INSIGHT
EDITIONS

PO Box 3088
San Rafael, CA 94912
www.insighteditions.com

f Find us on Facebook: www.facebook.com/InsightEditions

🐦 Follow us on Twitter: @insighteditions

ISBN: 978-1-64722-624-4

Publisher: Raoul Goff
Associate Publisher: Vanessa Lopez
Creative Director: Chrissy Kwasnik
VP of Manufacturing: Alix Nicholaeff
Senior Designer: Judy Wiatrek Trum
Editor: Samantha Holland
Editorial Assistant: Harrison Tunggal
Managing Editor: Maria Spano
Senior Production Editor: Katie Rokakis
Production Associate: Deena Hashem
Senior Production Manager, Subsidiary Rights: Lina s Palma-Temena

Photography by: Ted Thomas
Food & Prop Styling by: Elena P. Craig
Assistant Food Styling by: August Craig
Photos of Ashley Eckstein by Preson Mack; Instagram @pmack99
Hair and makeup for Ashley Eckstein by Ana Rivera, Beaute Speciale Inc.
Models: Freya, Harrison, Henry, Violet, Zennon

"One with the Force Breathing Exercise" photo on page 13: Disney/ David Roark

National Children's: Evidence-informed educational resources provided by On Our Sleeves®, the movement for children's mental health, powered by the behavioral health experts at Nationwide Children's Hospital

Insight Editions, in association with Roots of Peace, will plant two trees for each tree used in the manufacturing of this book. Roots of Peace is an internationally renowned humanitarian organization dedicated to eradicating land mines worldwide and converting war-torn lands into productive farms and wildlife habitats. Roots of Peace will plant two million fruit and nut trees in Afghanistan and provide farmers there with the skills and support necessary for sustainable land use.

Manufactured in China by Insight Editions

10 9 8 7 6 5 4 3 2 1

FEBRUARY 2023